Contents

MEDICAL PRACTICE MANAGEMENT

Body of Knowledge Review

VOLUME 9

Risk
Management

Geraldine Amori, PhD, ARM, CPHRM

Managing Editor

Lawrence F. Wolper, MBA, FACMPE

Medical Group
Management
Association

Medical Group Management Association
104 Inverness Terrace East
Englewood, CO 80112-5306
877.275.6462
Website: www.mgma.com

Production Credits

Executive Editor: Andrea M. Rossiter, FACMPE

Managing Editor: Lawrence F. Wolper, MBA, FACMPE

Editorial Director: Marilee E. Aust

Production Editor: Marti A. Cox, MLIS

Page Design, Composition, and Production: Boulder Bookworks

Substantive and Copy Editor: Sandra Rush, Rush Services

Proofreaders: Scott Vickers – InstEdit, and Mara Gaiser

Fact Checking: Mary Mourar, MLS

Cover Design: Ian Serff, Serff Creative Group, Inc.

PUBLISHER'S CATALOGING IN PUBLICATION DATA

Amori, Geraldine.
    Risk management / by Geraldine Amori ; managing editor Lawrence F. Wolper. – Englewood, CO : MGMA, 2006.
    117 p. ; cm. – (Medical Practice Management Body of Knowledge Review Series ; v. 9)
Includes index.
ISBN 1-56829-239-2
    1. Risk management. 2. Medical offices – Risk management. [LC] I. Wolper, Lawrence F. II. Medical Group Management Association. III. American College of Medical Practice Executives. IV. Series. V. Series: Body of Knowledge Review Series.

R728.A46 2006
658.562.A46—dc22   2005938863

Item 6362

ISBN: 1-56829-239-2   Library of Congress Control Number: 2005938863

Printed in the United States of America
10 9 8 7 6 5 4 3 2 1

Series Overview

THE MEDICAL GROUP MANAGEMENT ASSOCIATION (MGMA) serves medical practices of all sizes, as well as management services organizations, integrated delivery systems, and ambulatory surgery centers to assist members with information, education, networking, and advocacy. Through the American College of Medical Practice Executives® (ACMPE®), MGMA's standard-setting and certification body, the organization provides board certification and Fellowship in medical practice management and supports those seeking to advance their careers.

■ Core Learning Series: A professional development pathway for competency and excellence in medical practice management

Medical practice management is one of the fastest-growing and most rewarding careers in health care administration. It is also one of the most demanding, requiring a breadth of skills and knowledge unique to the group practice environment. For these reasons, MGMA and ACMPE have created a comprehensive series of learning resources, customized to meet the specific professional development needs of medical practice managers: the Medical Practice Management Core Learning Series.

The Medical Practice Management Core Learning Series is a structured approach that enables practice administrators and staff to build the core knowledge and skills required for career success. Series resources include seminars, Web-based education programs, books, and online assessment tools. These resources provide a strong, expansive foundation for managing myriad job responsibilities and daily challenges.

■ Core Learning Series: Resources for understanding medical practice operations

To gain a firm footing in medical practice management, executives need a broad understanding of the knowledge and skills required to do the job. The Medical Practice Management Core Learning Series offers "Level 1" resources, which provide an introduction to the essentials of medical practice management. As part of the learning process, professionals can use these resources to assess their current level of knowledge across all competency areas, identify gaps in their education or experience, and select areas in which to focus further study. The *Medical Practice Management Body of Knowledge Review Series* is considered to be a Core Learning Series – Level 1 resource.

Level 1 resources meet the professional development needs of individuals who are new to or considering a career in the field of medical practice management, assuming practice management responsibilities, or considering ACMPE board certification in medical practice management.

Also offered are Core Learning Series – Level 2 resources, which provide exposure to more advanced concepts in specific competency areas and their application to day-to-day operation of the medical practice. These resources meet the needs of individuals who have more experience in the field, who seek specialized knowledge in a particular area of medical practice management, and/or who are completing preparations for the ACMPE board certification examinations.

■ Core Learning Series: Resources to become board certified

Board certification and Fellowship in ACMPE are well-earned badges of professional achievement. The designations Certified Medical Practice Executive (CMPE) and Fellow in ACMPE (FACMPE) indicate that the professional has attained significant levels of expertise across the full range of the medical practice administrator's responsibilities. The Medical Practice Management Core Learning Series is MGMA's recommended learning system for certification preparation. With attainment of the CMPE designation, practice executives will be well positioned to excel in their careers through ACMPE Fellowship.

Preface

DESPITE VIEWPOINTS TO THE CONTRARY, risk management is not a function but a process.[1] It is a key process for business and is essential to protect the assets of the health care organization. These assets are not just the direct financial assets that could be endangered by a lawsuit, but also the intangible assets of lost opportunity, loss or diminished capability of personnel, loss or diminished usability of property, and the ever elusive loss of reputation and community trust.

Historically, risk management in health care has focused on losses incurred through medical malpractice.[2] Although certainly seen in most large, obvious losses, medical malpractice is only one component of the risk management process. In recent years, the focus has moved from clinical risk management, concentrated on losses directly related to clinical care, to a broader perspective. This perspective, known as enterprise risk management, considers all aspects of the organization's function as integrated components of overall loss exposure. Furthermore, in this framework, "risk" is synonymous with "capital." Risk exposure is therefore a direct potential loss of capital. Capital losses can come from operational exposures, financial risks, human capital risks, strategic risks, legal exposures, and technological risks.[3] In this risk management framework, the notion of risk management as a process tool rather than a "function" is not only reasonable, it is obvious.

Given that risk management cannot be relegated to a set of specific pieces of information, but must be examined by parts of the process, this volume first examines the risk management process and then addresses the skills and tasks related to its effective execution.

Learning Objectives

AFTER READING THIS VOLUME, the medical practice executive will be able to:

1. Describe the risk management process, including its goals and objectives;

2. Identify the skills identified for effective risk management and the components of the process to which they apply;

3. Be able to relate the various risk management tasks to their relationship in the process;

4. Continually assess potential medical practice risks to prevent malpractice suits, loss control issues, and government claims of abuse;

5. Communicate consistently to medical practice staff via the most appropriate media the commitment to minimize risk and maximize compliance to ensure high-quality patient care;

6. Interpret government regulations on corporate compliance, fraud, and abuse to physicians and staff to promote adherence;

7. Recognize the importance of reporting regularly to the board, administrators, and staff on risk-related matters to ensure an up-to-date understanding of liability issues for the practice; and

8. Investigate all claims against the practice and its physicians and staff to ensure patients and staff are treated correctly.

OSHA Inspection Nightmares

Tales of recent OSHA inspections

A SMALL MEDICAL PRACTICE IN MICHIGAN – ABC Clinic* – sustained hefty fines when a disgruntled employee complained to the Occupational Safety and Health Administration (OSHA) that her employer had not switched to safety needles. While OSHA found the practice was out of compliance in several areas, the staff's handling of the inspection actually racked up the fines. Why? When an OSHA inspector arrived unannounced at ABC Clinic, he was greeted warmly by the receptionist. After showing his credentials, he asked to be escorted to the clinical area. The staff allowed him to wander freely around the practice! Three hours later, the inspector left with a briefcase full of citations amounting to several thousand dollars. The physicians and staff were shocked two weeks later when they received a 15-page list of penalties. The group wrote a check to OSHA that week.

In another case initially related to safety needles, a practice employee at ABC Group in California accidentally pricked with a contaminated needle called the local OSHA office and lodged a formal complaint against her employer, which had previously refused to offer safety needles to employees. OSHA soon visited the office and discovered more than $40,000 worth of violations. The employer negotiated to get the fines reduced by $20,000.

*Names changed to protect the identity of the practices

In a different type of case, a disgruntled employee in Idaho called OSHA, reporting that his employer, ABC Family Practice, didn't have an OSHA manual and that patient areas weren't disinfected often enough. The surprised employer received a three-page letter from OSHA containing the employee's allegations and demanding a written response and copies of all applicable OSHA policies.

OSHA has inspected thousands of physicians' offices in the last few years. The most common citations were for violations of the Bloodborne Pathogens Standard and the Hazard Communication Standard.

What would happen if an OSHA inspector visited your medical practice today? Practice administrators must continually assess their offices' potential risks to prevent malpractice suits, loss control issues, and government claims of abuse and noncompliance. Risk management is an integral part of mastering the art of the medical practice executive's job.

Risk Management and the General Competencies

THE RISK MANAGEMENT DOMAIN within the *ACMPE Guide to the Body of Knowledge for Medical Practice Management* requires all five general competencies – (1) Professionalism, (2) Leadership, (3) Communication Skills, (4) Organizational and Analytical Skills, and (5) Technical/ Professional Knowledge and Skills – to be in place for a medical practice executive to be successful.

No aspect of the medical practice executive's job is exempt from the risks associated with the areas of compliance, security, liability, quality assurance, and patient satisfaction; keeping a keen eye on these areas is of utmost importance in risk management. In actuality, this is true not only for medical practice executives, but for physicians, clinicians, and staff as well.

■ Professionalism

The medical practice executive's approach to professionalism must include mastering the body of knowledge that supports the profession and its ethical and practice codes. Risk management involves every person within the practice who has any contact with patients, payers, referring physicians, vendors, and even the community at large. All members of the organization require a constant flow of information, data, and resources to successfully perform their responsibilities in a professional manner. A core set of procedures, policies, and practices forms the framework to guide the staff. The professionalism evident in how that information is managed, administered, and carried out by the practice executive sets the culture of the medical practice. The issues of fairness, consistency, equity, legality, justice, morality, and ethics all get rolled up into how professional the organization is in handling its people – staff, physicians, patients, and payers.

A medical practice can purport to have an inclusive set of risk management policies and procedures, but if it isn't administered and managed professionally, the practice suffers from a perceived lack of integrity and respect and is setting itself up for possible attack. Professionalism should be a core value for all medical practices, woven into the fabric of each organization. This commitment to professional standards allows the organization to carry out its risk management skills in the most effective manner.

■ Leadership

Leadership of the organization – setting and controlling its strategic direction – is an incredibly risk-intensive responsibility. Without good risk management resources and practices, leaders can fail in the current marketplace. The ability to predict and analyze risk within financial statements or governance structures takes a keen leader. This professional's attention must be focused on the business environment, competitors, regulatory agendas, and other strategic issues at all times.

The medical practice executive's role is pivotal to the viability of the medical practice. The Risk Management domain requires the executive's leadership to negotiate and comply with contractual arrangements; establish patient, staff, and organizational confidentiality policies; and develop and implement quality assurance and patient satisfaction programs. This type of leadership is essential to build the relationships needed to enhance and support risk management initiatives and opportunities. The Risk Management domain requires the medical practice executive to maintain an environment that fosters teamwork, accountability, and cooperation. It means that the physicians must work to develop effective processes through education, training, and problem solving, and the leadership must support the organization toward its vision and the implementation of that vision.

■ Communication Skills

Communication is the art and science of expressing and exchanging ideas in speech or writing. The intricacies of life require that the medical practice executive master both oral and written communication skills. In the Risk Management domain, communication is key to all parties – the person delivering the communication as well as the person receiving it – with an emphasis on understanding what is being communicated.

Risks are inherent in communication at all levels within the practice. A message (e.g., regarding compliance or confidentiality) can be misinterpreted or misunderstood because of a lack of clear communication. Sometimes information is not organized logically, or perhaps emotion overshadows a situation so that clear, objective information is not shared among physicians, staff, and patients. It is the responsibility of the practice manager to reduce the risks associated with such miscommunication.

The effective dissemination of information by the medical practice executive requires masterful communication skills. Whether information is communicated informally in face-to-face encounters or formally in speeches to large groups, whether in simple e-mails or in published memos and policies, presentation is crucial to understanding. The content of the communication can be diminished, or even destroyed, by a poorly conceived format or delivery style. The challenges in the Risk Management domain are to identify the most appropriate communication vehicles for the identified audience and to support whatever dialogue needs to occur to answer questions, seek clarity, and resolve conflict, thus averting the risk factor in communication.

■ Organizational and Analytical Skills

Organizational and analytical skills must be applied to convert the ocean of data that is collected or created in a medical practice to usable form. Until the information can be used for decision making, it has no value to the organization. The abilities to critically evaluate risk management-related information and to apply logical and analytical methods to create knowledge and understanding are among the most important job skills in a medical practice executive's repertoire.

Whether it is determining contractual compliance, studying liability trends and fraud and abuse reports, developing conflict resolution and grievance procedures for patients and staff, or conducting audits to evaluate at-risk financial dealings, risk management demands an orientation to and the mastery of organizational and analytical skills.

One of the most important (but most egregious accounts-payable items) is malpractice insurance. Knowing how to manage, evaluate, and communicate the importance of this line item requires an orientation to collecting and analyzing relevant information from multiple sources, discerning the salient data, and making sound decisions. Risk management requires the practice executive to interact with people, but the communication cannot be effective without solid organizational and analytical skills. These skills help the executive manage practice resources and work to achieve consensus regarding best performance.

■ Technical and Professional Knowledge and Skills

The *technical and professional knowledge and skills* associated with any profession are embodied in a collection of documented work. These bodies of knowledge are being captured in a variety of electronic media at an increasingly rapid pace. Accessing and navigating the profession's knowledge base requires the ability to use information technologies.

Running a medical practice requires a special set of technical and professional knowledge and skills unlike those for any other profession. The diversity and variety of situations that occur in a medical practice make its management type unique. A medical practice executive is expected to have a general knowledge of many areas along with a capacity to handle detailed information in many specific areas. Risk management techniques are inherently tied to the ability to create and manage documents and, more importantly, to efficiently access and evaluate the right kind of information at the right time. This involves not only organizational skills, but also technical and professional knowledge skills.

■ Summary

This volume is dedicated to reviewing each task associated within the Risk Management domain of the *ACMPE Guide to the Body of Knowledge for Medical Practice Management*. The medical practice executive's role requires proficiency and aptitude in all five general competencies, and the knowledge and skills found inside the Risk Management domain (within the Technical and Professional Skills and Knowledge competency) are critical for the success of both the practice executive and the medical practice. By learning and mastering this domain, the practice executive will glean the skills required to effectively lead the organization toward success.

Current Risk Management Issues

■ The Risk Management Process

To fully appreciate the ramifications and breadth of issues involved in risk management, it is essential to understand the risk management process.

Risk management as a process has four essential components:

1. *Risk assessment and analysis* – identification and analysis of exposures;

2. *Loss control* – identification and selection of potential mechanisms for addressing those exposures;

3. *Risk financing* – using selected techniques including risk financing, for failed control of losses; and

4. *Monitoring* – continuous monitoring of selected methods for controlling losses for potential improvement.[4]

These components applied to financial, human, operational, property, technological, and strategic areas across all aspects of the organization create the constellation that defines the organization's risk management program. What this means for the medical practice executive is related to the executive's ability to assess risks.

■ Risk Assessment and Analysis

The medical practice executive must ensure that s/he is aware of all potential risk exposures. As James Reason discusses in his book *Human Error*, every process contains latent errors, many of which are identified as such because our systems rely on consistently perfect human activity.[5] In fact, many processes depend on human vigilance and omniscient foresight to stop errors from occurring. Examples on a grand scale include the lack of coordination of resources early in the 9/11 tragedy and, more recently, the disorder that resulted in the loss of lives and chaos after Hurricane Katrina.[6] On a smaller, but still significant scale are those preventable failures that result in medication errors, fires on site, staff injury, failures of service initiatives, or loss of business productivity due to technology failures. In each of those circumstances, the blame often is laid on the person who "didn't follow the policy" or "didn't pay close enough attention." In fact, processes without risk control mechanisms to counter the human factor are fraught with latent errors. The opportunities for error can become aligned through serendipitous occurrences, or through a series of small human errors that can ultimately result in devastating outcomes and losses. Reason's "Swiss Cheese Model," often quoted in patient safety literature, is applicable to all aspects of an organization's processes and activities. The alignment of any number of process "holes" can result in risk management exposures. The key is to find where those latent exposures lie before losses occur. [7]

Ultimately, the most exhaustive way to identify potential exposures in complex systems is through a process, such as a failure modes and effects analysis (FMEA). This process, which gained popularity through its use in engineering, is designed to examine every step of a process and identify the myriad ways in which each step could fail, as well as the potential for that failure to be stopped.[8] Nevertheless, even a tool as powerful as FMEA is limited by resources. Such analyses take time. Obvious loss potential areas may justify the dedication of human capital for this type of intensive analysis. Nonetheless, many processes have the potential to lead to equally devastating losses. How then does an organization priori-tize the processes to review?

Information on exposures that have high loss potential can be gathered from a number of sources. The organization's own insurance claims and malpractice loss runs are basic sources of information. Complaints from patients and/or staff are another fundamental source of information. Formal risk assessments by outside consultants, self-assessment questionnaires, literature reviews, and insurance application forms also provide exposure identification. Furthermore, by examining the questions on the insurance application or survey forms, the executive can ascertain which processes are perceived as high risk by insurers and other surveyors. Finally, by using a simple but effective technique, staff can list the various processes in each department and then ask "What can go wrong?" for each process. If answered honestly, it will be apparent from the list where loss control mechanisms might be useful.

■ Loss Control

The next step in the risk management process is to analyze the data and identify the tools that will reduce either the frequency (loss prevention)[9] or the severity (loss reduction)[10] of losses. The potential losses prime for application of these techniques are (1) those that occur frequently even though the cost per loss may be small (e.g., missed appointments or employee unplanned absences); and (2) those that occur infrequently but are more costly per loss (e.g., medical malpractice claims). Furthermore, as stated earlier, any process that relies heavily on human compliance with complex procedures (or procedures in a complex environment) is subject to great variability and potential error.

Those areas in any process in which high variability or high potential for loss exists should be addressed first. Potential methods to address these issues can be found in the industry literature or through insurance or business consultants. Nonetheless, a key point to remember is that loss control methods are not uniformly applicable in all situations. The unique location, culture, and characteristics of each organization may render a solution a potentially bad fit. Consequently, each considered solution must be analyzed for its potential latent failures in the given situation.

Planning and Preparedness for Catastrophic Events

Losses stemming from natural disasters provide examples of the variability needed in loss control methods. Flood and emergency evacuation processes that worked in Vermont in the ice storm of 2000 were not uniformly applicable to New Orleans in 2005 in the face of Hurricane Katrina. Both were water- and wind-based disasters. Both affected the availability of electricity and potable water. Both affected transportation. Both created temperature conditions that were dangerous to humans (the ice storm resulted in deaths by freezing and collision; the hurricane in deaths by drowning and heat). Both required evacuation of vast numbers of people from nursing homes and hospitals. However, unlike the aftermath of Katrina, the New England ice storm did not result in potential infectious disease through coliform or mosquito transmission, and it did not result in the decay of human remains. In addition, the repair time and the time before people could return to their homes after the ice storm was shorter. Although there certainly is much to be learned from the communication among agencies, the military, and first responders such as emergency service personnel, many other aspects of the emergency plan do not go far enough to meet the needs of a different type of water- and wind-based disaster.

In addition to natural and human-made disasters, increasing attention is being paid to the threat of an influenza pandemic. Medical practices should review disaster preparedness protocols and procedures in their organizations and in their communities to be up to date on the incorporation of pandemic influenza preparedness into emergency management procedures and what their own roles and responsibilities would be at that time.

The Department of Health and Human Services (HHS) and the Centers for Disease Control and Prevention (CDC) have published a number of resources specifically targeted to help medical offices and ambulatory clinics assess and improve their preparedness for responding to pandemic influenza. Medical practices may find that they need to adapt the information and checklists to meet their unique needs.

Given the rapidly changing nature of pandemic influenza information at the federal, state, and local levels, medical practices should monitor the Websites of the HHS (www.hhs.gov/pandemicflu) and CDC (www.cdc.gov/flu), as well as other selected Websites for new and updated information. The Website www.pandemicflu.gov contains links to state pandemic influenza emergency plans, which medical practice leadership and staff should review and use to complement their overall plan.

According to the CDC, medical offices should develop a structure for planning and decision making. The structure should include a planning committee with both clinical (physicians, nurses, and ancillary staff) and administrative (medical practice administrator and support staff) representation, as well as the services of an environmentalist, if possible. One person in the organization, such as the practice administrator, should be assigned responsibility for coordinating preparedness planning for the practice. A point of contact (either someone in the clinic or an outside consultant) should be responsible for answering questions and/or providing consultation on infection control to prevent transmission of pandemic influenza. The organizational structure should be described in a written pandemic influenza plan.

The plan developed for the practice should be consistent with existing practice emergency/disaster plans and with community response plans. The key elements of an influenza pandemic plan for prepared medical practices are:

- A plan for surveillance and detection of pandemic influenza in the population served;

- A communication plan;

- Provision for an education and training program to ensure that all personnel understand the implications of, and control measures for, pandemic influenza;

- Informational materials for patients on pandemic influenza, which are language and reading-level appropriate for the population being served, including a means to distribute these materials[11];

- A plan for triage and management of patients during a pandemic;

- An infection control plan[12];

- A vaccine and antiviral use plan; and

- An occupational health plan has been developed that addresses issues related to surge capacity (i.e., dealing with an influx of patients as well as a shortage of staff and supplies) during a pandemic.[13]

In these extreme examples of actual and potential disasters, the same principle applies to any proposed loss control solution. No loss control mechanism should be selected without full consideration of the influence of local cultural and environmental conditions on the potential for failure. Even apparently fail-proof plans may fall short due to unforeseen events. The World Trade Center buildings were built to withstand potential encounters with airplanes. However, the World Trade Center was built many years before the Boeing 767s, which ultimately hit the towers, had even been designed.[14]

High Reliability Organizations

In the risk management selection process, consideration should be given to developing procedures that increase a system's reliability. This should include any mechanism that reduces variability through human fatigue or physical condition, variance in the physical environment, and reliance on human vigilance. The concept of the High Reliability Organization (HRO), originally studied at the University of California at Berkeley, is being applied throughout clinical care organizations to address the issue of providing care in complex systems under complex conditions.[15] Although based on industries for which safety is a key issue, such as aviation or nuclear energy, high-reliability concepts also apply to health care processes, where error can also result in significant loss.[16]

HROs have certain characteristics that contribute to consistent outcomes. Among the most salient are their flexibility when it comes to decision making and organization. Whoever has the information or appropriate skill can assume responsibility as the situation dictates. Bureaucracy is adaptable to the needs at hand. Furthermore, HROs are obsessed with reliability to the point of trumping efficiency. Their culture communicates and supports the value of reliability, and it rewards people for exhibiting the desired behavior in critical situations. Finally, organization employees are taught to maintain awareness of the situation and to make efforts to understand situations that do not seem right, rather than to ignore them or to assume that it is the job of someone higher on the administrative level, and they are reinforced in these efforts.

Along with these traits are tools that are designed to reduce variability in action by reducing reliance on vigilance, memory, or habit. Those tools include checklists, clearly defined procedures that are supported by reminders and lists, task simplification to reduce the number of steps, a reduction in the number of hand-offs, and automatic correction on critical steps.[17] It is impossible to predict everything, however. Given that, it is essential that appropriate risk financing be available to cover unforeseen losses.

■ Risk Financing

Most executives are familiar with the risk-financing vehicles of commercial insurance and self-insured vehicles, such as captives, risk retention groups, and trusts. What many executives may not fully appreciate, though, is that commercial insurance, although more costly, is effectively a contractual transfer of risk.[18] The risk of loss belongs to the insurer. Consequently, the risk of financial devastation through catastrophic events is minimized for the organization. The downside to risk transfer is that the insurance company maintains control over what will be covered and retains the ability to increase premiums. Furthermore, the premium paid by the organization is not based solely on the organization's history nor specifically on its loss control efforts, but on an aggregate of similar organizations with combined loss experience. Of course, some attention is paid to the organization's specific loss history; however, the cost of overhead and need for margin to the insurance company sometimes outweigh those benefits.

Risk transfer is not bad. For forms of losses that are unpredictable and potentially costly (e.g., automobile, directors' and officers' liability, employment liability, property, key person), commercial insurance is the standard and probably most cost-effective form of risk financing. The organization hopes to never need it. Nonetheless, it would be extremely difficult to predict ultimate losses and to plan for setting aside sufficient funds to cover these losses should they occur.

Self-insurance vehicles are best when there is a known frequency and consistent value of typical losses.[19] The organization must have sufficient funds set aside to cover those losses. Self-insurance vehicles tend to be less expensive to administer and offer the organization more control over the loss control mechanisms and their effect on the premium.

In addition, there are losses that occur infrequently but result in such large losses that it is better to cover them with more structured forms of risk financing. For minimal losses or extremely infrequent losses, risk financing might include loans, nonfunded reserves, or even payment from the operations budget.

Given the variety of options for risk financing, it is essential that the medical practice executive understand the full array of potential risks faced by the organization and plan accordingly for failure in any arena. Does the organization have a plan to respond to a disaster that affects all technological equipment? Is there a plan should delivery of medical supplies be cut off? Is there a plan for a loss of water or electricity, for a contagious illness reducing the availability of staff to care for patients, or for severe weather resulting in patients and staff being forced to remain in the building for days? What is the plan should an intruder hold staff hostage? The number of risks that must be provided for and covered both through procedures and possible risk-financing mechanisms is seemingly unlimited.

■ Monitoring

Time changes all things. The methods and procedures that work at one time can suddenly no longer fit the organization's practice. The challenge is to remain attuned to the influence of organizational change on loss control methods. Once a method of loss control is chosen, the tendency is to be so desirous of it working that signs that it is not working are ignored. Monitoring and reevaluation of all loss control methods, therefore, must occur regularly.

Standardized times should be scheduled for review of written policies and procedures as well as actual processes as performed in the organization. A standard timetable for review will ensure that the organization is regularly updating all aspects of its risk management program.

Knowledge Needs

ACCORDING TO ACMPE, there are 10 key skills, or knowledge needs, required of the medical practice executive for effective execution of the risk management process. Those skills can be grouped in alignment with the steps of the process described in the previous chapter.

Risk Assessment and Analysis Skills

1. Continually assess potential medical practice risks to help avert malpractice suits, address loss control issues, and deter government claims of abuse.

2. Interpret government regulations on corporate compliance and fraud/abuse issues and inform physicians and staff to promote adherence.

3. Negotiate contracts (including capitation agreements) with payers, contractors, vendors, and other outside resources to eliminate risks for the practice.

Loss Control Skills

4. Communicate consistently to medical practice staff via the most appropriate media the commitment to minimizing risk and maximizing compliance to ensure high-quality patient care.

5. Build and maintain a relationship with legal counsel to ensure the most appropriate resources on practice liability matters.

6. Plan security systems and training to minimize possible workplace violence in the medical facility.

7. Write and communicate clear policies on medical practice risk and compliance matters, including medical records, self-referrals, and patient safety, to limit risk exposure.

8. Investigate all claims against the practice, its physicians, and staff to ensure that all parties are treated fairly and correctly.

Risk-Financing Skills

9. Report regularly to the board, administrators, and staff on risk-related matters to ensure up-to-date understanding of liability issues for the practice.

Monitoring Skills

10. Evaluate future risks for the practice in light of past history, present conditions, and forecasted trends to ensure adequate preparation for the future.[20]

Clearly, there is overlap and redundancy in the risk management process. Monitoring skills are also assessment skills. Risk-financing skills are part of monitoring skills as well as risk-reduction techniques. It is not reasonable to expect the medical practice executive to possess all of the skills required of a risk manager. However, it is reasonable to expect the executive to recognize any discrepancy between his or her personal skill set and the required skills for the job and to seek the services of a professional risk manager if needed. Most important, the medical practice executive should have a firm grasp of all loss exposures faced by the organization and be able to recognize when the resources for addressing those exposures may have to be sought from outside the organization.

Overview of Risk Management Tasks

WITHIN EACH OF THE SKILLS identified in the previous chapter are numerous tasks. ACMPE has designated 11 risk management tasks for the medical practice executive, which correlate with the identified skills. Within each of those tasks are correlated knowledge components supporting those skills.[21] The next part of this volume examines each task along with its knowledge base.

Medical practice executives should develop and use their knowledge and skills to ensure that the following tasks related to risk management are carried out.

■ TASK 1: Maintain legal compliance with corporate structure

From legal relationships to legal liability, and from risk management strategies that incorporate corporate compliance and communication plans, this task allows the reader to develop an understanding of the various legal aspects that must be followed based on the practice's corporate structure.

■ TASK 2: **Maintain corporate history and develop record-keeping procedures**

Corporate records are legal documents that must be maintained in accordance with pertinent state and federal laws and regulations, which, in turn, may vary by state and jurisdiction. Accordingly, it is essential that the practice's risk management plan address retention, storage, and retrieval policies for such documents. This task introduces the reader to the components and factors necessary to develop a system to properly maintain records and comply with the law, thus averting risk for the practice.

■ TASK 3: **Develop conflict resolution and grievance procedures**

The relationship between an employer and employee is complex at best. Conflict is often unavoidable; legal counsel should be involved in any negotiations, and accurate records of all interactions should be kept on file as a risk management strategy. Whether needed for process improvement or for litigation, unbiased, complete documentation supports the organization's adherence to policies and procedures and is evidence of fair action. This task covers the mediation process, grievance procedures, and complaint investigations.

■ TASK 4: **Assess and procure liability insurance**

From malpractice and officer liability insurance to loss ratios and loss experience, this task presents an overview of how underwriting and contract negotiations are handled and why practice administrators are wise to employ an experienced, qualified insurance broker with expertise in health care to ensure that the organization appropriately addresses financing mechanisms for identified risk exposures.

■ TASK 5: **Establish personnel and property
security plans and policies**

It is incumbent on employers not only to be fair and nondiscriminatory in hiring and terminating employees, but also to take responsibility in providing a safe work environment. A number of laws and regulations apply to protecting personnel. This task covers policies and procedures related to workplace violence, patient confidentiality, OSHA, the Fair Labor Standards Act of 1938 (FLSA), sexual harassment, investigation tactics, and monitoring techniques.

■ TASK 6: **Develop and implement quality assurance
and patient satisfaction programs**

This task relates to the key issues of creating and maintaining an effective quality assurance program in the medical group practice setting. In addition, this task covers why a goal to provide the best patient care and just the right amount of it is ideal to minimize risk exposure.

■ TASK 7: **Establish patient, staff, and
organizational confidentiality policies**

Confidentiality for patients as mandated by the Health Insurance Portability and Accountability Act of 1996 (HIPAA)[22] and the inherent risk of a breach of that confidentiality are among the major risk factors for the medical practice manager. This task involves HIPAA's privacy and security regulations, which limit the type of protected health information that can be disclosed, to whom it can be disclosed, and how it can be disclosed, as well as outlining the steps needed to secure electronic health information at rest and in transit. Staff and organizational confidentiality also carry risks, so education regarding all confidentiality, whether mandated by HIPAA or not, is an essential part of the medical practice executive's risk management arsenal.

■ TASK 8: **Conduct audits of at-risk financial activities**

Just like personal income taxes, the tax codes that apply to businesses change regularly. This task outlines why the medical practice executive should stay abreast of the organization's risks by regularly running accounting and cost analysis reports, applying industry comparisons for benchmarking, and keeping apprised of any ongoing continuing-education courses and reading material that is available.

■ TASK 9: **Develop professional resource networks for risk-related activities**

Every practice has a wealth of internal knowledge and expertise. However, few practices have the knowledge and expertise to handle every business, legal, and financial issue that arises. This task shows the administrator how to develop appropriate professional resources and how to recognize those high-risk areas where outside consultants may be most useful.

■ TASK 10: **Negotiate and comply with contractual arrangements**

As this task shows, contract negotiation is a multifaceted activity. Contracts create legally binding obligations between two parties (e.g., a payer and a physician), and every contract is unique and requires careful consideration. This task highlights the nature of the contract and dictates the components that are most critical for risk management.

■ TASK 11: **Maintain compliance with government contractual mandates**

This task addresses the numerous laws and regulations regarding compliance with government contractual mandates and their application to the practice. Understanding and embracing these laws will help to ensure that staff members comply with specific laws related to the reporting of activity, the nature of contractual relationships, and the regulations pertaining to employees and employment, all areas that carry risk exposure.

Maintain Legal Compliance with Corporate Structure

BY FAR THE MOST FREQUENT AND SUBTLE EXPOSURES for any organization are those created by legal and regulatory bodies. The proliferation of legislation relevant to health care fills volumes far beyond the capacity of this guide. Furthermore, the complexity of legislation, regulation, and standards creates an opportunity for multiple interpretations or misinterpretations and misinformation that subject most organizations to scrutiny or allegations, even in the face of self-perceived appropriate behavior. There is no reasonable way to avoid exposure. A basic knowledge of laws and regulations, a healthy uncertainty about what constitutes compliance, and a good relationship with a trustworthy attorney are key elements toward building a case for due diligence and good faith effort should the organization's actions be called into question.

■ Knowledge of Federal, State, and Local Laws and Regulations

Many federal, state, and local laws and regulations affect health care organizations. General corporate and business laws affect the structure and operation of medical organizations. Among those are the tax laws that apply to the corporate structure selected by the organization. Certainly the size of the organization and its anticipated growth as well as tax goals and concerns about liability will affect the structure selected by the principals.

Structure of the Organization

A practitioner who does not intend to work with a group may elect to form a sole proprietorship, which is the simplest form of business. The drawback to this structure, however, is that the physician assumes personal liability of the business, thereby risking loss of personal assets. More formal structures, such as limited liability corporations (LLCs), provide more protection, and they have gained popularity with sole practitioners and very small group practices.

The C-corporation, a flexible structure popular with large group practices, offers more protection while allowing physicians to own stock in the company. This flexibility, however, does not come without a cost. In essence, the stockholders are taxed twice. The corporation is taxed on its income, and then the shareholders are taxed on the income they receive from the corporate income. Although less structurally flexible, a popular corporate structure is the S-corporation. Under this structure, personal liability is limited and the corporate profits flow to the shareholders as taxable income.[23]

Commensurate with the actual legal structure, which may or may not require a board of directors, the tax status (profit or nonprofit) will also affect applicable laws, activities, and physician compensation plans for compliance.[24,25] Furthermore, many corporations consider creating foundations as separate legal entities to support charitable activities. Foundations may be supported by individual donor gifts or corporate donations. Strict regulations govern foundations, including tax regulations. The decision about corporate and tax structure, as well as the establishment of a foundation, is best made with guidance from legal counsel. The organization must have a clear picture of both its growth and tax goals to make the appropriate decisions.

Collaborations

At times, competitors may collaborate for specific projects or services to enhance their ability to offer a service. Collaborations are different from mergers in that most competitor collaborations are usually time-limited, and competition continues in all areas except those affected by the collaboration. In those situations, the relationship is defined by contract, and the parties must ensure that the collaboration does not create antitrust issues.[26] Guidelines for preventing antitrust issues in a variety of joint ventures and other collaborative relationships have been developed jointly by the Federal Trade Commission (FTC) and the U.S. Department of Justice (DOJ) in a document called *Antitrust Guidelines for Collaborations Among Competitors*, an important resource for the health care executive.[27]

Even more than antitrust concerns, kickbacks and Stark law violations are concerns in collaborative relationships. The anti-kickback statute[28] does not permit a provider to "knowingly or willfully solicit, receive, offer, or pay remuneration for services paid for under any federal health care program."[29] Simply stated, this statute prohibits goods or money from being given in exchange for referrals. It is easy to see how this could happen innocently in a collaborative relationship: One party agrees to provide the other with office space, a share of profits from medications, durable medical equipment, or services in exchange for referrals to a specific program. The anti-kickback statute carries both criminal and civil penalties. Although there are exceptions, such as "safe harbor regulations," it is prudent for the organization to have an attorney familiar with the subtleties of this law review any contracts that establish relationships.

Similarly, the Stark regulations (I and II) prohibit referral by a provider to any entity in which the provider has a financial relationship. Known as the "Ethics in Patient Referrals Act," Stark I was promulgated in an effort to deter referrals to substandard providers. It also was intended to prohibit overutilization or unfair competition. Stark II broadened regulations to include Medicaid patients and all designated health services (not just lab services)[30] and was passed in an effort to clarify the provider self-referral prohibitions. Both Stark regulations carry civil penalties.[31] These related but distinctly different issues of corporate compliance create dilemmas about appropriate behaviors and business arrangements that must be carefully considered in negotiating collaborative relationships.

Other Laws

Other laws may apply to the medical practice, depending on the size of the practice and the corporate structure. Organizations that receive federal funding may be subject to laws such as the Drug-Free Workplace Act, which requires the employer to notify employees of the regulation prohibiting the use, distribution, manufacture, or possession of controlled substances in the workplace.[32] Other key regulations that may apply include the following:

- *Occupational Safety and Health Act of 1970* – established the Occupational Safety and Health Administration (OSHA). OSHA is committed to safe work environments. It promulgates regulations and conducts inspections. Regulations apply under specific circumstances and organizations are monitored for compliance.

- *Americans with Disabilities Act of 1990 (ADA)* – expanded the Rehabilitation Act of 1973, which protects handicapped employees. ADA prohibits discrimination against an individual based on major life impairments (disabilities) if a person is otherwise qualified for a job. Employers are mandated to make reasonable accommodations to comply with this regulation. In addition, this law establishes standards for accessibility of new or renovated construction.

- *Family and Medical Leave Act of 1993 (FMLA)* – provides that private-sector employers with more than 50 employees provide up to 12 weeks of unpaid job-protected leave for medical reasons. This act applies only to employees who have worked more than 1,250 hours over the preceding 12 months.

- *Employee Retirement Income Security Act of 1974 (ERISA)* – allows employers to determine the medical costs of their own group and to self-fund the risk of employee medical costs. In addition, the act provides that the employer is not subject to premium tax or mandated benefits.[33]

■ Legal Relationships

Laws and their associated implications are insidious. It is easier to be in violation of a legal nuance than to be certain that you are in compliance. Furthermore, with the rapid proliferation of legislation at the federal, state, and local levels, and the recent focus on patient safety and patient rights, it is quite possible for statutes in the same jurisdiction to conflict in some areas. Even within state laws, conflict can exist or be perceived to exist when interpreted by different legal entities.

Consequently, it is essential for the medical practice executive with risk management responsibility to have a relationship with a respected law firm known to be both ethical and efficient. The practice will want an attorney who is familiar with general legal principles and general business issues. This may be an attorney who serves as the gatekeeper or the central point for ensuring there are no conflicts generated among the specialists. This attorney may also be the one who watches out for the best interests of the organization in a general way, keeping an eye on the changes in local, state, or federal law that may be of interest to the organization.

In addition, the practice should engage attorneys specifically trained in environmental issues, medical malpractice, compliance, employment law, and contract law. (Some attorneys may specialize in more than one of these areas.) The medical practice executive will want to work with each of these specialists and coordinate their work to ensure conflicting perspectives are not being generated that will create inadvertent additional risk exposure for the practice.

With so many attorneys, though, it could be easy to spend all the savings from averting risk exposure on attorney fees. It is therefore essential that the medical practice executive understand how legal fees are generated and monitor the billings. The wise professional will ensure that s/he has an understanding of the legal system and how it works, client rights, and the benefits of lower-cost methods to resolve legal disputes, such as mediation and arbitration. By fully understanding one's rights as a client, as well as the avenues available to the attorney to resolve disputes, the medical practice executive can function as a "partner" in the legal process rather than a passive recipient of services.

Leadership Liability

In the past, it was considered a privilege to serve on the board of an agency or organization. There were few exposures and many benefits. The tide has now changed, however, and boards and officers of corporations are being held personally accountable for their decisions and their actions.

Boards of directors can no longer accept the word of leadership at face value. There is a public duty to conduct due diligence efforts, which include speaking up on issues, recognizing the responsibility to dig beneath the information presented to ensure its validity and veracity, and recognizing that the board members may be held accountable for civil or even criminal penalties if they are found to be derelict in their responsibilities.

Officers and directors are not only responsible for the direct fiscal decisions of leadership, but also accountable for ensuring compliance with all federal regulations and statutes through the corporate compliance plan. They are also responsible for ensuring that the organization does not engage in unethical or illegal conduct in relation to federal funding agencies, including the Centers for Medicare & Medicaid Services (CMS) or granting agencies, and that tax number usage, billings, and contracts are legal and free of anti-kickback or Stark implications. Furthermore, the board and officers have oversight responsibility with regard to structural changes in the organization, including partnerships, mergers, de-mergers, and collaborative relationships.

A director or officer cannot hold office in name only. For example, in 2005, the chief executive officer (CEO) of a large medical center in the Northeast was sentenced to two years in prison because of his efforts to circumvent state Certificate of Need regulations. The CEO believed he was innocent because he felt his actions were justified. The officers of the organization, including the chief operating officer and chief financial officer, were also tried. The board of directors was dismantled and pled innocent to knowledge of the activity, saying they had taken the word of the officers at face value. They were spared charges. It could have ended differently, and in the future it might.

Any individual who chooses to serve on the board – or as an officer in a health care organization – should carefully weigh the risks and the benefits. It is an honor to serve, but it is also a legal and fiscal responsibility. The ethical organization will ensure there is sufficient directors and officers (D&O) liability insurance and that the directors are aware of their personal liabilities beyond the limits of the D&O coverage. The members of the board must have a clear understanding of their personal responsibility for conducting due diligence on decisions they make as well as a complete understanding of the vulnerability of their records and conversations under the rules of discovery. Finally, it is the duty of the organization to ensure that directors are educated on their responsibilities regarding all legal requirements for the organization so they can discharge their duties both effectively and appropriately.[34]

Assessment and Decision Making

Although most formal claims will be managed by a claims manager, the medical practice executive must have a working understanding of the implications of pursuing litigation as opposed to settling or finding alternative resolution approaches. Once allegations have risen to the level of a claim, there will be financial ramifications, regardless of whether that claim goes to litigation. Although litigation offers the possibility of victory (in which case no indemnity is paid to the plaintiff), there are still costs in the form of attorney fees, court costs, experts, and other discovery expenses, as well as organization costs in the form of staff and administration time and resources. In a small claim or a claim that is obviously an error,

nobody wins when litigation is pursued. In cases where it is obvious that there is no wrongdoing or negligence (e.g., medical malpractice) under the law, litigation may be the best route.

Litigation is almost always an expensive and protracted process.
Other forms of determination are available. In addition to settlement outside of court, alternative resolution processes such as arbitration and mediation provide less adversarial and time-consuming
mechanisms for coming to agreement in disputed situations.
Arbitration can either be binding, meaning that the parties must
adhere to the decision rendered, or nonbinding, meaning that the
parties are free to accept or reject the opinion rendered and pursue
litigation. In contrast to arbitration, mediation involves a process
that is designed to bring both parties to an acceptable decision
without going to trial. There are many forms of mediation, which
generally are not binding; however, the goal is to reach agreement
on an outcome that is acceptable to both sides of the dispute.

Settlement of a claim, by contrast, is generally the submission
of the defendant to demands of the plaintiff to avoid the cost and
difficulties of a trial. There may be some negotiation of amounts
paid, but settlement is different from mediation in that it is not a
process designed specifically to meet the needs of both parties. In
fact, settlement is generally favorable to the plaintiff. In all situations, the cost-benefit ratio of going to court vs. avoiding court
must be based on the total cost of litigation compared to the damage created by conceding on any point of the accusation. If the
damage to the organization, either financially or in reputation,
exceeds the benefit of early resolution, then it is wise to pursue litigation. Many times, however, organizations choose to pursue litigation because of the insult of the allegation or the desire to be seen
as justified in their actions rather than making a decision based on
the ultimate ramifications. Each organization must develop its own
philosophy about litigation and alternative forms of resolution.

The philosophy of the organization regarding claims management is an essential part of the relationship with legal counsel.
Attorneys are usually paid by the hour (defense counsel) or contin-
gency (plaintiff counsel). Unless the medical executive is clear about
avoiding unnecessary litigation costs and has a philosophy of early

resolution when appropriate, legal costs will be a prominent part of the company budget. When working with attorneys, it is wise to develop retainer contracts that reward rapid resolution and use of legal resources commensurate with the organization's philosophy.

Governance Development and Policy Adherence

The practice's governance should ensure that policies and procedures are clear to avoid disputes about processes. Furthermore, the relationships among board members and between board members and staff should be clearly defined. Finally, the right to and methods for due process should be clearly delineated.

■ Risk Management Strategy

As stated earlier, risk management is a process, not a function. As such, the medical practice executive's perspective and focus on risk management depends on his or her belief system, values, and perceived organizational relative exposure. Nevertheless, for risk management to be effective, there should be a plan and a strategy to ensure that exposures are adequately identified and addressed.

There are many approaches to a risk management plan; however, certain elements are universal to all plans:

- Exposures should be addressed in the key areas of patient care, medical staff, employee relations, financial risks, property risks, and technological risks. Other types of risks the organization may have are technical, vehicular, and environmental. Any key area of the organization's operation should be addressed.[35]

- A system should be in place for financing potential losses.

- The board and leadership should be knowledgeable about exposures and losses and should be engaged in prevention.[36]

Although this volume has reinforced the notion that risk management is a comprehensive activity that includes all elements of the organization's function and processes, it remains true that the greatest exposure for significant ongoing financial loss for a health care organization is in the area of medical malpractice.

Given that, the strategy to address injury to patients is key to a successful risk management program. In patient care, as in every other aspect of the organization, the most effective way to control loss is to prevent it. That is the goal. Due to human variability and the vast number of services and procedures provided by medical organizations, however, it will be many years before all the latent errors currently in existence can be adequately addressed. By then, more errors will have emerged with the proliferation of new technologies, medications, and procedures.

A successful risk management plan must include a method to constantly monitor new exposures and address existing exposures in patient care. Staff should be included in the process in whatever ways are reasonable. The most basic level is reporting actual and potential errors. Every potential error is an opportunity to prevent a loss in the future because it exposes a latent failure in the system. Reporting systems that include near misses or potential loss events are key to an effective risk management plan. Other tools for assessment include loss runs from previous claims, surveys and assessment tools, and reports from outside consultants.

Reporting is not limited to situations of human error or process, however. It includes malfunction of medical devices, which include any device that is not a medication used in the process of treatment – from simple tongue depressors up through the most complex equipment. The Safe Medical Devices Act of 1990 (SMDA) requires that device users notify the manufacturer, or the Food and Drug Administration (FDA) if the manufacturer is not known, about any malfunction that involves serious injury or death of a patient.[37] Often the malfunction of medical devices is attributed by health care workers to "user error," or a work-around provides temporary remediation of the problem. In an effective risk management program, users are encouraged to report all events, including the duct taping of hoses or alarms that do not trigger, in an effort to forestall medical events that may be device-related. If equipment is involved in a claim, it should be impounded. Under no circumstances should it be repaired or returned to the manufacturer. It is key evidence should the claim proceed to litigation.

Peer review activity as a process for improving care is essential. Peer review activities, appropriately carried out, identify variability in the practice, which leads to less reliability in the system. It can also point out those providers who consistently achieve better than average results as well as those outliers who may require assistance. Peer review should not be used as a cloak to avoid transparency and truthfulness with patients. It should be used as intended – for physicians to monitor their peers to ensure and achieve a higher level of medical practice and care for patients.

Finally, the risk management strategy should include the organization's philosophy about claims management and investigation. Immediate investigation of a claim provides the best defense against fading memory and alteration or disappearance of evidence. In addition, early investigation provides the opportunity to identify the latent failures in the system that led to at least one patient injury, and could, if unaddressed, soon lead to another. Care should be taken to ensure that all discussions about the claim are protected under attorney direction as part of the claims investigation process. All original medical records should be locked so that no changes can be made to them. A copy of the record should be made and put into circulation for the continuing care of the patient.

The SMDA has limited application in the office practice setting. For example, physician practices are exempt from the law while ambulatory surgery centers and outpatient diagnostic and treatment facilities (e.g., chemotherapy and dialysis) must comply with it.[38] The professional in charge of risk management should be aware of the appropriate application for the setting in which care is being provided.

Corporate Compliance

Corporate compliance is an area that has confused many people due to the number and types of laws that are included in this seemingly catch-all area. In its simplest terms, corporate compliance is the organization's program to ensure that it meets all relevant federal and state laws as well as the program requirements of federal, state, and private health plans. In actuality, a compliance program includes this concept plus the formula for executing and running a compliance program defined by the Office of the Inspector General (OIG) plus the requirements of any number of agencies that have begun to monitor the health care system with regard to compliance.

The OIG-recommended compliance program elements are based on the Federal Sentencing Guidelines.[39] The OIG believes that every hospital and integrated health care delivery system, regardless of size, location, or corporate structure, should apply all of the following elements, modified to fit their unique situations:

- Development of written standards of conduct (often referred to as a "code of conduct");

- Continuing education of all staff on these standards of conduct;

- Development of written policies and procedures to promote the hospital's commitment to compliance (e.g., medical and business record policies, evaluation of managers on adherence to policies, and monitoring of necessity of care) and to address specific areas of potential fraud, including:

  - Incorrect reimbursement;

  - Record falsification;

  - Fraudulent billing and documentation practices;

  - Billing errors;

  - Inadequate documentation of care;

  - Continuation of unneeded or unauthorized care;

  - Inadequate patient information;

  - Client abuse;

  - Patient discrimination;

  - Inadequate safety plan for patients/staff; and

  - Inappropriate acceptance of gifts;

- Designation of a chief compliance officer charged with the responsibility for managing and monitoring the program;
- Ensuring the chief compliance officer has reporting and communication access directly to the board and the CEO;
- Designation of a corporate compliance committee;
- Creation and implementation of regular, effective education;
- Creation and maintenance of a reporting process, such as a hotline for complaints;
- Creation of a process for permitting and securing the anonymity of complaints and for protecting whistleblowers;
- Creation and maintenance of a system for responding to allegations of illegal or unacceptable actions;
- Definition and enforcement of disciplinary actions for employees who violate internal compliance policies or the applicable statutes, regulations, or requirements;
- Monitoring and auditing regularly to ensure ongoing compliance (including physician participation in medical record/billing audits); and
- Development of policies addressing the nonemployment or retention of individuals identified in the OIG exclusion list as sanctioned.[40]

A complete listing of compliance program guidelines can be found on the Website of the HHS Office of Inspector General in the "Fraud Prevention & Detection" section under "Compliance Guidance," available at: http://oig.hhs.gov/fraud/compliance guidance.html.

■ Communication Plan

For a risk management plan to be functional, it will include a structured mechanism for ongoing communication about exposures, policies and procedures, systems improvements, and unanticipated events. Key audiences for risk management communication include:

- *The board of directors*, which is ultimately responsible for the safety of patients and corporate compliance;

- *Administration*, which sets the corporate culture's tone. This tone either creates an environment in which reporting and action in the face of potential error are customary and free from retribution, or it establishes one in which safety and risk prevention take a back seat to efficiency and competition;

- *Physicians*, who must understand the corporate expectations and culture within which they are working;

- *Staff*, who take personal risks of retribution when they report an error or potential error and who must understand policies and how to implement them;

- *Patients*, who are called on as partners in today's system to help report potentially unsafe situations or events; and

- *The public*, who are the practice's constituents.

The communication plan for risk management should include both verbal and written communication. Written communication should consider the issue of medical literacy and be written so that laypersons and all staff, including support staff, can understand it. A comprehensive risk management communication plan will include:

- *Orientation presentations* for both the board and staff, including the role of risk management, the responsibility of the staff and board, and the types of risk management involvement expected of them. In addition, the orientation should communicate the philosophy of the organization about retribution-free reporting and the expectation that all staff and the board will participate in ensuring that the organization complies with established standards of safety and corporate compliance.

- *Regular written reports to the administration and board*, including claims, suits, events, near-misses, and identified exposures. In addition, written reports should include loss prevention and loss control activities as well as monitoring activities.

- *Regular written communication to staff* to apprise them of exposure and acknowledge them for reporting exposures. Staff are the eyes and ears of the risk management process. Unless they are rewarded for exposing risks, their participation will be limited. The effective risk manager will acknowledge and reward staff participation in risk management activities. In addition, staff need to know about actions taken in response to their reports.

- *Corporate communication* through writing for internal newsletters, which should be the responsibility of the risk manager whenever possible. The more widely the risk management activities are known throughout the organization, the more corporate support is possible.

- *An understanding of public relations*, especially careful verbal and written communications in situations with high potential for litigation, for example, those occurring after an unanticipated event. The goal of public relations is to create a positive image of the organization, and the risk manager must have an understanding of the implications for liability and legal ramifications. The need to contain speculations and protect patient confidentiality while providing sufficient information so as not to be deceptive or perceived as deceptive by the public is paramount.

All staff should be educated about the need to avoid hearsay and gossip about unanticipated events. Speculation is damaging. Random musings become facts in the minds of those who share them. All staff, not just clinical staff, should be trained on the concepts of systems thinking in medical error and the notion of high reliability as an organizational goal. The more educated staff are about safety thinking and the notions of corporate compliance, the more they can believe the organization is just, fair, transparent, and striving to improve safety, and the more they will grasp their role in damage control. Risk management can create plans, processes, and procedures; however, without communication of risk exposures, loss reduction plans, and results, there can be no risk management success.

TASK 2 # Maintain Corporate History and Develop Record-Keeping Procedures

■ Corporate Record-Keeping

Corporate records are legal documents that must be maintained in accordance with pertinent state and federal laws and regulations, which may vary by state and jurisdiction. Accordingly, it is essential that the risk management plan address retention, storage, and retrieval policies for such documents. Furthermore, the primary responsibility for ensuring proper storage and retention should include a designated backup should the process owner (e.g., the medical practice executive) be unavailable. Finally, the plan should include a loss control process for electronic backup of important documents. Under most circumstances, it is prudent to retain a copy of important documents at a location that is physically distant from the primary storage location. This should prevent any type of disaster from destroying all copies of significant information. Many organizations keep original documents for the length of the statute of limitations pertinent to the most likely allegations related to the document.

The types of documents that should be addressed in a risk management plan include, but are not limited to:

- *Articles of incorporation.* In addition to copies retained by the organization and the state of incorporation, a copy should be retained by corporate counsel.

- *Bylaws.* Original and current copies should be retained.

- *Bylaw changes and documentation.* A copy of previous versions of bylaws should be retained for documentation in case of litigation. In addition, it is prudent to keep redlined versions of approved changes to facilitate the tracking of changes.

- *Stock and/or outstanding shares.*

- *Minutes (board, committee).* At least two archive copies should be retained in segregated secure locations.

- *Employment agreements (physician, administrator, others).* These should be retained in accordance with applicable statutes.

- *General ledger.* Copies of the general ledger should be kept in accordance with applicable tax laws.

- *Corporate history.* Records of corporate history should be retained indefinitely in some retrievable format.

- *Medical records.* Different regulations and statutes apply to the retention of patient medical records and employee health or OSHA records. Patient medical records are generally retained in accordance with the statute of limitations for bringing malpractice action defined by the individual state. Employee records must be retained in accordance with the type of employee health services provided on site. For both types of records, the practice should confer with counsel familiar with the applicable statutes.

- *Physician credentials.* Physician credentialing records may be accessed, despite their presumed protection from discoverability, by a variety of sources: the Joint Commission on Accreditation of Healthcare Organizations (JCAHO), the physician if ever denied privileges, or a plaintiff who may allege negligent credentialing. Given those potentialities, credentialing records should be maintained for the maximum duration of the statute of limitations for bringing action against the hospital or according to record retention statutes of the state, whichever is greater.[41]

- *National Practitioner Data Bank (NPDB).* NPDB queries and reports should be kept along with and for as long as credentialing files. Litigation based on negligent credentialing or hiring, or alternatively, litigation alleging wrongful termination or denial of privileges that call into question reports to or from the NPDB, will likely shadow claims for wrongful termination or negligent credentialing practices.

- *Discovery documents on current litigation.* These documents are important throughout the litigation and appeals process. It is generally prudent to retain records for seven to ten years after litigation in case a related case emerges. Records will likely be retained by counsel, and extended retention may not be required.

■ Computer Aids for Recording History

Less than 30 years ago, record-keeping was limited to rooms filled with boxes of materials stored where mold, dust, mice, and dampness could destroy them. Today, computers provide the opportunity to maintain records in electronic formats so that environmental changes cannot affect them and space for storage is reduced to a minimum. In addition, computer programs provide the opportunity to format information in standardized ways that are accessible and usable by a variety of people.

Common computer programs include databases that are designed to store many records of a similar nature in a retrievable format. Often databases generate reports that sort and list records that contain specific fields. In addition, spreadsheet software is used universally to display and analyze numerical data and financial records. Presentation programs are used to display reports in a readable format, and word processing programs are used to generate documents. Although in the past many brands of these programs of these types were not compatible, in recent years the trend has been toward creating programs that can "talk" to each other in common formats. The benefit of using these types of programs for record-keeping is the universality of access. Almost any computer user with a PC-compatible operating system can access, read, and modify records as needed. However, this capability also creates a vulnerability exposure for unauthorized changes to records.

Redlining changes in documents is an effective risk management tool for policies and procedures and other documents that are regularly revised. Redlining marks changes within the document so it is clear when alterations occurred. In litigation, policies and other records are often requested for production during discovery. The presence of redlined documents allows the organization to prove that it is producing the version of the document in use at the time of the alleged malpractice or other allegation.

E-mail is considered an official record in the context of litigation. It is increasingly being demanded as part of the discovery process. The danger of e-mail, though, is the very characteristic that makes it easy to use. The anonymity and informal nature of e-mail tends to elicit casual comments and speculation from writers. These unbridled communications could cause damage in litigation. Staff should be cautioned about the official nature of business communication via e-mail. It should not be used for speculation, gossip, or threats.

■ Record System Organization

Despite modern tools, electronic records are not free from destruction. Operating systems change, computer programs and compatibilities change, accessibility to older forms of data storage change, and data may be lost. In addition, computers can break down or can be damaged by water or fire. The same loss control mechanisms as for hard copies of important documents, including redundancy of storage, storage in a variety of formats, and segregation of copies, are essential.

In addition to the safeguards of physical separation and redundancy of files, a variety of individuals should have access to the files. It is often prudent to also keep the source documents (such as paper forms) for a period of time commensurate with state regulation. Transcription errors, disputes about the validity of the documentation, and allegations of misrepresentation are likely to arise in the early life of a document. Historical documents provide a framework for decisions but may be called on more rarely in litigation.

TASK 3 **Develop Conflict Resolution and Grievance Procedures**

■ Labor and Administrative Law

The relationship between an employer and employee is complex. In exchange for employee effort and commitment, the employer provides financial remuneration and protections of certain kinds. Although the employee's formal relationship is with the employer as an entity, the actual relationship is with supervisors and co-workers at the local working level. Those relationships color the employee's perception of the employer and can lead to interactions and issues that require intervention. Sometimes employees are not suited to the work and act out in ways that require disciplinary action. Sometimes human relationship problems exacerbate the significance of work issues.

Historically, the lack of policies to protect employee rights coupled with abuse of the employer–employee relationship led to the formation of employee unions around the turn of the 20th century. Since then many laws have been promulgated that further define the rights of both parties. Despite the best intentions, employees and their supervisors may perceive corrective actions differently.

At-will employment does not remove employer responsibility for providing grievance procedures. Statutes and regulations that support grievance procedures for employees include:

- *National Labor Relations Act of 1935 (NLRA)* – defines labor practices for both employers and employees that are unjust; provides mechanism for complaint hearings; defines mechanisms through which employees can select a union.[42,43]

- *The Fair Labor Standards Act of 1938 (FLSA)* – sets maximum hours and minimum pay for employment.

- *Weingarten rights* – offer employees the right to have a co-worker or union representative present during an exploratory interview that might result in disciplinary action. These rights prevent the employer from purposefully creating barriers to the co-worker's presence through willful schedule changes or workload demands; however, the employer is not constrained to make more than a reasonable endeavor to schedule the interview at a time that is unproblematic for the co-worker.[44,45] Although Weingarten rights originally applied to union employees, in 2000, the National Labor Relations Board (NLRB) ruled that nonunion employees were entitled to the same rights.

- *Equal Pay Act of 1963* – amends the FLSA; prohibits sex discrimination with regard to wages.

- *Title VII of the Civil Rights Act of 1964* – prohibits employment discrimination of any kind on the basis of race, color, religion, sex, or national origin.[46]

- *Age Discrimination in Employment Act of 1967* – protects employees over the age of 40 from age-related employment discrimination.[47]

- *Equal Employment Opportunity Act of 1972* – amends Section 706 of the Civil Rights Act of 1964 and applies to private, state, and local government employers; it prohibits hiring discrimination on the basis of sex, age, religion, race, color, or national origin.[48]

- *Americans with Disabilities Act of 1990* – prohibits employment discrimination based on major life impairments, such as hearing disabilities or visual disabilities. If a candidate is otherwise qualified, an employer must make reasonable accommodation to avoid discriminatory action.

In addition to the federal laws regulating employment, states have specific laws that cover labor relations, union relations, child labor, and workers' compensation. It is incumbent upon the medical practice executive to be fully apprised of applicable laws for the corporate structure, tax status, and size of the medical practice.

Whenever possible, it is prudent risk management to settle disputes at the lowest possible level, which means before litigation. Mediation, which is the use of a trained professional who serves as a conduit for dialogue between the parties with the goal of achieving agreement, is a proactive and positive approach for dispute resolution. Another form of alternative dispute resolution is the use of arbitration. Arbitration involves a third party who is empowered by the court to make a decision after weighing the evidence on both sides of a dispute. Arbitration may be binding (the parties must adhere to the decision rendered) or nonbinding (the parties do not have to adhere to the decision rendered), depending on the jurisdiction and the contractual agreements between the parties. (Also see Task 1 for information on mediation and arbitration.)

In all cases, it is incumbent upon the organization to ensure that either termination of employment or disciplinary action is based on progressive warnings with defined, fair, and progressive avenues for resolution of disputes. Although employers should strive for fair and effective hiring and management processes, employees must be provided an unbiased outlet for expression of concern about perceived breaches of fair practice.

Note that in a unionized organization, the medical practice executive should be very careful not to cross the boundaries of union law. Where there is union activity or if the staff is unionized, prudent risk management includes consultation with a lawyer familiar with union activity.

■ Grievance Procedures

Separate and distinct grievance procedures are mandated for a variety of situations. Federal regulation demands internal processes for handling grievances related to workplace issues, including sexual discrimination and perceived improper treatment of whistleblowers.[49] In addition to employment-related grievances, a number of other situations require formal processes for resolution.

For example, the CMS Conditions of Participation (CoPs) require health care organizations to have internal processes for handling patient complaints about care. These CoPs include complaints about the quality and adequacy of care, access to care, and termination or refusal of care. Internal processes must be unbiased and have progressive levels of appeal.[50]

In addition, insurance denials, part of operations in a complex insurance structure, require internal processes for investigation, remediation, and resolution. Insurance denials may be due to billing errors, bad timing, improper referral processes, or incorrect billing formats. Payment may also be denied or delayed by patients. In many situations, the potential is high for negative interpersonal and legal interactions. In some cases, patient satisfaction can be sufficiently affected to precipitate litigation if coupled with unsatisfactory outcomes or care. Consequently, expeditious determination depends on timely, reliable, and effective processes. Relationships and cash flow depend on effective resolution mechanisms.

How grievances are handled internally is often a matter of administrative structure and policy. Regardless of the details about how a grievance is processed or to whom it is submitted, there are basics that apply to all grievance processes:

- There must be a nonpunitive method to report grievances. Anonymous hotlines or online reporting are encouraged as nonpunitive ways for employees and patients to report concerns about treatment.

- The process must be fair. The employee or complainant who chooses to be identified must be assured that there will be no ramifications for registering a complaint. This can be tricky.

Patients hesitate to complain because they may feel the provider will consciously, or subconsciously, label them. Employees are sometimes afraid to complain because they feel they will be singled out as troublemakers and jeopardize their position in the organization.

- The process must include fair representation. Representation may not necessarily be a lawyer, but may include a co-worker, a family member, or other appropriate party, depending on the situation.

- The process must include recourse if there is no satisfactory resolution.

■ Complaint Investigations

A complaint is a significant event in the organization. Although some complaints are unfounded, many contain an element of truth. The truth may be convoluted by the individual perspective of the person who is complaining; however, the behavior, action, or activity at the root of the complaint represents an exposure for the organization. After full investigation, it may be tempting to dismiss any complaint not proven to be outside the confines of expected behavior as a misunderstanding or disgruntlement.

A risk management perspective is to evaluate the factors that led to the complaint and recognize within them the latent exposures. There could be system exposures that render billing difficult to accomplish appropriately in certain circumstances, or processes that depersonalize patient interactions or create the potential for a breakdown in communication. Perhaps staff patterns of interacting create the potential for allegations of sexual misconduct. Even where the legal "bullet" is dodged, the potential for future exposures remains great.

Recommendations for investigation of grievances and complaints are similar to the suggestions for investigations of alleged malpractice. Investigations should occur promptly after a complaint is received, while memories are fresh and the conditions are most like they were at the time of the alleged action. At that time, it is hoped that data have not been altered in any way. Furthermore, any information impounded shortly after the complaint is less subject to allegations of alteration because it is out of circulation.

The first step is fact finding. This can occur through retrieving appropriate records, talking with individuals involved in the situation, and questioning those who may know something about the situation. Wherever possible, impound not only records, but also equipment, computers, medical devices, or other tangible items involved so that tampering, whether intentional or unintentional, cannot occur and thereby affect litigation evidence.

The next step is to identify all of the applicable federal and state laws and regulations. If a complaint is made under a specific federal mandate, such as the ADA or sexual harassment, then an applicability determination should be made by legal counsel. Risk management, even when the risk manager is an attorney, is not the practice of law. Effective risk management involves a working knowledge of the applicable statutes and regulations, but does not presume to interpret them officially. It is essential that a complaint involving legal ramifications be handled in conjunction with legal counsel. Certainly the medical practice executive handling the investigation should be able to render a perspective and a personal interpretation of the applicable statute or regulation; however, final definitive interpretation should be done by assigned counsel. If the risk manager is also in-house counsel, then it is important to be clear about what role is being performed at any given time.

Once the facts and legal ramifications are clear, it is essential that solid conflict resolution skills be used with the complainant. Regardless of the validity of the complainant's perspective, nothing said about the law or the intention of the alleged perpetrator will change the complainant's personal perspective. What is possible to achieve is peace through agreement to restore the dignity of the person who is complaining. Most complaints are ultimately about personal dignity. Here skilled intervention is recommended. The use of trained mediators is often highly successful in bringing about resolution.

In situations involving actual wrongdoing on the part of the organization or its agents, prudent risk management action involves providing appropriate restitution to the aggrieved party. Again, legal counsel should be involved in these negotiations, and records of all interactions should be kept on file. Proper documentation of all aspects of the process and investigation are key. Whether needed for process improvement or for litigation, unbiased, complete documentation is evidence of adherence to policies and procedures and to fair action.

TASK 4 **Assess and Procure Liability Insurance**

THE HEALTH CARE ORGANIZATION is a complex network of exposures. Some exposures can be easily managed and controlled, and some are more insidious. Latent exposures may pass unnoticed until a loss occurs. Furthermore, some exposures are conducive to self-insurance mechanisms, whereas others are better served through commercial insurance. An experienced, qualified insurance broker with expertise in health care is the best counsel to ensure that the organization appropriately addresses financing mechanisms for identified risk exposures.

■ Insurance Requirements and Products

Each medical practice has its own unique needs. A practice with a great deal of computer equipment might want or need a specific rider to cover that equipment. A practice that has a swimming pool to provide physical therapy may have specific coverage for that. In general, the types of insurance listed below denote the most common types of insurance coverage for a group medical practice:

- Professional liability (medical malpractice);
- General liability;
- Property and casualty;
- Directors and officers liability;

- Workers' compensation (which is not an employee benefit, but a risk control coverage);
- Key person (in small practices);
- Employment liability;
- Environmental;
- Vehicle;
- Helipad (if the organization has one); and
- Business interruption.

The selection of insurance products can be overwhelming. Which product offered by which company will provide the best coverage for the organization's specific needs? Would a self-insured vehicle best meet the organization's financial and exposure needs for all or part of the medical malpractice or workers' compensation coverage? As with any major investment, all parts of the insurance relationship should be evaluated.

Many organizations work with a broker to help procure quotes and make decisions. An insurance broker is different from an agent. An agent represents a single insurance company. Any insurance bought from that individual will be from his or her company. Using an agent may limit the flexibility in coverage that the practice may want. A broker is trained to evaluate the needs of the client and the insurance market. The role of the broker is to find the best coverage for the client's unique needs. Furthermore, the broker has a relationship with the insurers recommended. A broker can negotiate with underwriting to ensure the client is given the best deal possible for the exposures being insured.

The role of the underwriter is to assess the exposure the health care organization brings to the insurer as the recipient of the risk transfer. The underwriter compares the organization's loss potential with that of similar organizations functioning in similar venues. With that baseline, the underwriter then looks at the specific loss history of the organization to determine the level of risk posed. By using actuarial formulas, the underwriter determines the premium. Other costs are added to the premium based on the insurance company' overhead as well as the services provided by the insurance company.

A skilled broker can also advise the client if self-insurance is in the client's best interest. Working with the broker and an actuary, the organization can conduct a feasibility study. Sometimes the practice will be approaching readiness for self-insurance, but is not yet ready to take the leap. A broker can design an interim insurance program that will allow the practice to assume part of the risk before taking the plunge into full self-insurance.

■ Risk/Benefit Analysis

Even with a skilled broker, the medical practice executive should be prepared to ask questions and to challenge recommendations. To do this, the executive has to have a handle on the risks and benefits of each type of risk-financing vehicle or policy presented. The executive must understand the cost of risk in the organization and have answers to questions about the present coverage such as: What insurance coverage is currently in place? What are the limits of coverage? What are the deductibles, both by claim and aggregate? What are the attachment points for each layer of coverage? What losses have been paid from operations, through loans or through unfunded reserves, during the last five years? Are they losses that should have more formal financing to take advantage of present dollar value?

Once the medical practice executive understands the current cost of coverage, s/he should review the actual practice losses for the last 5 to 10 years. Where did losses occur? Which were the frequent small losses and the less frequent large losses? Were there any unexpected losses? Are there potential losses identified through the risk-assessment process that have not yet occurred, but could be devastating to the organization if they should occur? Are there insurance or self-insurance vehicles to prepare for them?

With this information, the executive has a picture of the coverage in place and the exposures that have resulted in losses. The benefits and drawbacks of each type of insurance product must then be weighed. As discussed earlier, the benefit of commercial insurance is that it is known coverage. The limits are defined in the policy, which is a contract of risk transfer between the medical practice and the insurer. The downside of commercial insurance is its overhead and profit loading. The services that are "included" are also included in the premium. Although this might make self-insurance appear to be the only reasonable route, that is not true for every exposure. The cost of some services, such as claims management or risk management, may exceed the rate in the premium. Furthermore, self-insurance requires oversight and administration. The decision to self-insure or to purchase commercial insurance is one of philosophy, convenience, and financial capacity.

◼ Organizational Commitment

Regardless of the type of risk-financing vehicle selected, the organization benefits from tight loss control processes. The temptation to diminish loss control when there is commercial insurance must be avoided. When the insurance market is tight and there is very little competition for customers, those practices with the best loss records and the tightest loss control methods will be the ones with choices regarding an insurer. Those with few processes may find insurance difficult to procure.

Reduction of loss exposure is not just the job of the person with risk management responsibility. It requires commitment on the part of the board and administration to provide the necessary resources for loss control. It further requires that physicians understand the benefit of loss control methods to their practice and that time spent participating in risk management activities may directly relate to less time spent defending their practice in court. Finally, all personnel must realize that risk management is the job of each person in the organization. Although attributed to insurance, true risk management is about people, patients, and staff, as well as maintaining a fiscally viable organization so that the people who work there will continue to have a place to work and to serve others.

TASK 5 **Establish Personnel and Property Security Plans and Policies**

▪ Federal, State, and Local Laws and Regulations

Not only is it incumbent on employers to be fair and nondiscriminatory in hiring and terminating employees, employers also have a responsibility to provide a safe work environment. A number of laws and regulations apply to protecting personnel. The Fair Labor Standards Act requires employers to pay all nonexempt employees no less than the state minimum wage and requires $1\frac{1}{2}$ times the minimum rate for those who work more than 40 hours a week.[51]

In addition, the Equal Pay Act of 1963 prohibits differences in pay between men and women who perform "substantially equal jobs" unless those differences are due to some factor other than gender, such as merit pay, seniority, or training.[52] These laws refer to the protection of employees from unfair advantage by the employer. Similarly, Title VII of the Civil Rights Act of 1964, which includes actions of sexual harassment, applies not only to the actions of employees and their supervisors, but also to patient interactions with staff, or staff-to-staff interactions. According to the Civil Rights Act, "sexual advances, requests for sexual favors, and other verbal or physical conduct of a sexual nature constitute sexual harassment when this conduct explicitly or implicitly affects an individual's employment, unreasonably interferes with an individual's work performance, or creates an intimidating, hostile, or offensive work environment."[53] This act implies that the employer has a duty to provide protection from psychological harassment or unwanted sexual advances in the workplace.

Through the Americans with Disabilities Act, the employer is charged with protecting the employee from discrimination because of life impairment that otherwise does not interfere with the ability to perform the job.[54] The Occupational Safety and Health Administration is charged with creating standards for physical safety in the workplace. The duty of OSHA is to "assure safe and healthful working conditions for working men and women; by authorizing enforcement of the standards developed under the Act; by assisting and encouraging the States in their efforts to assure safe and healthful working conditions; by providing for research, information, education, and training in the field of occupational safety and health; and for other purposes."[55,56]

Violence is an increasing concern in the health care workplace.[57] The employer has a duty to protect the employee from discrimination or unfair advantage not only by those within the organization, but also by others not necessarily controlled by the practice. Because the employer cannot assume that the source of violence will be known in advance, every practice should have a security plan that includes controlled access to the office, staff ability to monitor the entire waiting area, sufficient staff to de-escalate an emergency, 911 programmed into all phones, locked access to pharmaceuticals and other potentially desirable goods, and rehearsed drills for dealing with violent patients or intruders.[58] In addition, OSHA has generated recommendations for protecting health care workers against workplace violence. These recommendations are not OSHA regulations or standards; they are in response to the recognition that health care workers serve the public in ways that are emotionally charged and consequently are at risk for violent actions.[59, 60]

■ Policies

When developing policies, the medical practice executive should ensure that security policies are comprehensive. These policies should address violence or potential danger from a variety of sources, including disruptive physicians, visitors, staff, patients, family or friends of staff, and intruders. Systems should be in place to address a variety of situations and, wherever possible, alliances with local law enforcement should be made in advance of an actual emergency. Although it is important for all practices to have a security plan, practices with known risks should regularly perform drills to test proposed policies and procedures. Obvious risk exposures that generate the need for simulation drills include on-site medications, in-office procedures or surgeries, high-risk locations, known substance-abuse or emotionally disturbed patients, and evenings or weekend hours of operation. Clearly, most practices would benefit from a comprehensive security plan and commensurate simulation drills.

It is essential not only to have a plan and policies, but also a staff that is trained, retrained, and continually trained. Emergencies should be rehearsed regularly. Documentation of planning, training, and rehearsal should be maintained.

■ Monitoring Techniques

Risk exposure monitoring must happen on a regular and ongoing basis. It is essential that the medical practice executive understand the limitations and demands of both federal and state laws that apply to employees, premises liability, and visitors. Furthermore, to protect the organization, the medical practice executive should be conversant on state-permitted use of property surveillance, permissible drug testing of employees, and permitted use of pre-employment physicals and reference checks.

Recipients of federal funds are mandated to comply with the Drug-Free Workplace Act of 1988, which requires employers to have a drug-free awareness program and drug-free policies. Employees must be aware that drug use, manufacture, or distribution is not permitted in the workplace. Furthermore, any convictions related to drugs must be reported to the employer. The act, however, does not mandate drug testing.[61] Drug testing and surveillance are guided primarily through state laws.

The ADA and the Civil Rights Act address reference checks and pre-employment physicals. Employee policies should be reviewed by an employment attorney prior to implementation. Employees have certain rights to privacy of their information,[62] so there should be limited access to employee personnel files. In addition, medical files, drug testing (where applicable), and information related to medical conditions and/or bloodborne pathogen exposure should be kept apart and secured away from regular files. Furthermore, any records related to attorney communication about an employee or involving litigation should be retained separately with limited access.[63] Employees should be apprised of the organization policies regarding employee confidentiality at orientation, and these policies should be reinforced regularly with all staff.

■ Patient Privacy Protection

Policies must include employee responsibility to maintain the confidentiality of patients. Training on the privacy rules of the Health Insurance Portability and Accountability Act of 1996 (HIPAA) should be part of each employee's orientation and repeated regularly. Risk management has revealed that the most frequent violation of patient privacy occurs when the patient is a fellow employee. Because employees have access to medical information through computerized systems, it is tempting for a caring colleague to "check up" on a friend, which violates HIPAA regulations.

Another potential abuse of patient privacy by staff involves the use of computerized information to gather personal information. For example, in one hospital, an employee with an otherwise immaculate record used the computer to locate her estranged husband, who was living with a new partner. In the process, the employee became intrigued with the health status of the husband's new partner, and discovered she was pregnant. The employee lost perspective on the nature of her actions, and when the new partner learned that the employee knew of her condition, she lodged a complaint about breach of privacy. Disciplinary action was taken against the employee, who did not deny the action and was jolted back into recognizing her wrongful activity. Employees must be told and reminded that their right to access information about another person, whether a colleague, family member, or acquaintance, is based on a job-related need to know, and that any other use is a violation of patient privacy.

HIPAA is only one part of patient privacy protection. In many states, the physical presence of a patient on the premises of a health care organization is not, of itself, considered confidential or protected information. This is not true, however, for patients in designated substance abuse treatment programs, who are protected by federal statute,[64] and this is also not true for mental health programs in many states. Regardless of state protection, it is an unwise practice to acknowledge patient presence in the health care office. Unlike an inpatient facility, where the patient has the opportunity to opt out of the patient directory at admission, outpatients are generally not asked their preferences for acknowledgment of their presence. Consequently, it would not be difficult for disgruntled partners, angry acquaintances, estranged spouses, and noncustodial parents to track a potential victim of verbal or physical violence to the physician's office. Staff should be trained to cautiously handle calls from and the physical arrival of such persons. Scripts that do not validate the presence or absence of the patient should be developed and rehearsed. Messages should be taken from the visitor and delivered by staff to the patient, who can then decide whether to allow the person to know of his or her presence in the office. The unanticipated arrival of a spouse or parent bearing a concealed weapon cannot be underestimated. Staff should be trained that patient safety is a priority and that careless management of patient information is grounds for disciplinary action.

**Develop
and Implement
Quality
Assurance
and Patient
Satisfaction
Programs**

■ **Capitation Contracting**

Capitation contracting is a form of contracting that is
fraught with potential exposures. There are basically two
types of capitation contracts, each of which has its own
set of exposures. With delegated capitation contracts, the
provider receives the monthly capitation allowance in
advance and uses it to pay for services provided. The
advantages of this type of contract are that the practice
manages the time delay between the receipt of monies
and services provided, and it creates a more timely access
to funds. At the same time, however, delegated capitation
contracts can create a cash-flow problem for the provider
organization, which must be able to cover any member's
medical costs within the constraints of the monthly allo-
cation. By contrast, in a nondelegated capitation contract, the managed care plan functions more as a
traditional health insurer and pays for services as they are
provided. At the end of the agreed-upon contract period,
the practice and the plan reconcile the performance and

settle the monies.[65] Both methods have benefits and drawbacks, and they both require quality assurance and utilization oversight.

Capitation contracts should be read very carefully with an eye to protection of the rights of patients and the practice. In addition to the financial considerations in the contract review, factors related to quality assurance and patient satisfaction considerations include:

- Services covered under the plan and considerations for how the organization will provide or address services that are not covered with patients;

- Credentialing requirements for providers and peer review considerations;

- Contractual inducements for limiting care, and the organization's processes for ensuring that financial inducements to limit care do not take precedence over the provision of quality care;

- Contract termination duties to the managed care organization and the provider organization's policy and plan for treating and/or transferring patients covered under the plan without risking abandonment or patient dissatisfaction;

- The managed care plan's desired access to records (both medical and business);

- Actual cost to the practice to treat patients in the rated categories vs. the rate being paid per patient;

- Liability and hold-harmless clauses (e.g., the insurer attempting to shift liability for any action or nonaction on its part to the practice); and

- Whether the extent to which the conflict resolution process is delineated by the contract disadvantages the provider in relation to providing care to the patient.[66]

■ Quality Management and Utilization Management

A goal of patient care is to provide the best care and just the right amount of it. Quality management and utilization management processes within the practice have tremendous impact on the cost of services and the outcomes. Triggers for quality management should include any of the exposures in patient care identified during the risk assessment. Each is a potential quality area where patient care is compromised. Furthermore, standard triggers for quality review include sentinel events, repeat admissions within 30 days, and health care-acquired infections, among others. Issues of quality are identified in many ways. Standard event reports and patient complaints are sources of quality information. Furthermore, billing denials and attorney letters of inquiry provide clues to issues of utilization or quality care. Quality improvement should not be a reactive function in post-problem identification, but rather a proactive part of the risk management process to identify problems before they become events.

For quality to be an integral part of the care process, staff must be trained to recognize and report both actual events and situations where systems or processes result in compromised patient safety or care. The organization must have an infrastructure that supports ongoing process improvement through dedicated staff who are trained in process improvement techniques including root cause analysis and failure modes and effects analysis, as well as through resources for making and monitoring recommended changes.

Utilization management ties into the quality process through monitoring practice patterns and patient visits and admissions. Outlier practice patterns, variation in service patterns, and changes in admission and discharge patterns are all indicators of potential quality or process concerns.

■ Patient Satisfaction

Patient satisfaction is a time-honored, long-appreciated, but not often a well-understood factor considered in the improvement of care. Although patient-satisfaction surveys query specific issues such as waiting room time, politeness of staff, or even parking convenience, these surveys primarily measure satisfaction with human interaction. From a patient's perspective, care that is given respectfully and communicated well is care that is appreciated and well perceived.[67] Patient satisfaction measurement tools can provide great feedback for areas in which improvement in quality of processes can be applied, and where staff training on communication and interaction with patients and families will improve the overall relationship of the practice to its customers, patients, and families.

Many organizations use standardized surveys, available from vendors, such as Press Ganey, which allow for benchmarking against similar practices. Nonetheless, simple tools and phone surveys often yield even more pertinent and effective information. In addition to the traditional and important amenity queries about parking, staff politeness, timeliness, and facility, effective satisfaction surveys will measure perceptions of care appropriateness, thoroughness, and communication. In addition, queries about perception of safety and patient involvement in decision making are emerging as a result of the increased focus on patient safety and patient-centered care.

The goal of gathering data is to use it to make change. Patient satisfaction data are useless, however, unless they are used. Properly analyzed, such data hold the key to patient retention and reduced likelihood of litigation. Whatever the methods used by the organization to gather information about patient satisfaction, they should be used to spur change and pinpoint areas for improvement on an ongoing basis.

Data trends should be distributed to appropriate departments and individuals for corrective responses or celebrations of success. Such trends indicate where appropriate quality improvement efforts should be initiated. Customer service training, training in patient-centered care, patient flow processes, or other initiatives can all be monitored through response trends in patient satisfaction surveys. In all cases the data should be communicated with leadership and the board in addition to all staff at least quarterly.

■ Federal and State Laws and Standards Regarding Industry

Quality processes are governed by a variety of industry regulations and standards. In addition to the surveys provided by the Joint Commission on Accreditation of Healthcare Organizations (JCAHO), CMS and other accrediting and state agencies may monitor the health care organization for quality. The medical practice examiner should be knowledgeable about the specific organizations that conduct surveys and audits in the states where the practice has facilities. Whoever interfaces with regulatory agencies should remain apprised of changing regulatory information. This individual often seeks interpretation of regulation as it applies to the specific practices of the medical group, and distributes findings and works with the quality improvement process to facilitate change.

Peer review laws in many states protect quality records from discovery in an effort to ensure free communication about potential issues within the practice. Within that protection, peer review activity, credential files, and event reports are often considered protected information. In addition, many states have legislation and regulations that require reporting specified data elements for state monitoring. Some states are tracking specific disease categories; others may be monitoring treatment processes for specific diagnoses. Each state has its own specific laws regarding protection and reporting with which the medical practice executive involved in risk management activities must be familiar.

■ Malpractice Risks

Malpractice risks emerge in a variety of ways. Physicians who are incompetent or impaired are a grave danger to the practice for several reasons. Negligent credentialing and negligent hiring are potential allegations. An obvious risk is an untoward event involving patient injury. The reputation of the organization is also at risk due to the perceived tacit approval or acceptance of incompetent or impaired physicians. Although each of these risks is significant, incompetent physicians are not the only malpractice exposure. Poor prescription-writing techniques, including the use of unapproved abbreviations, indiscriminant prescribing of controlled drugs, or illegible handwriting, are significant risks of malpractice as well as patient safety issues. Physicians who routinely perform unnecessary procedures, either through erroneous clinical judgment or in an effort to maintain productivity levels, are a malpractice risk as well as a fraud and abuse risk. Diagnostic errors and their corresponding consequences, missed diagnoses, and misdiagnoses – all of which can lead to delayed or inappropriate treatment – are major sources of malpractice allegations. Often these types of errors are the result of human factors that contribute to missing a process or not recognizing a vital piece of information. Often, providers receive training in managing procedures and care in accurate and well-managed situations. Simulation and practice are generally inadequate, however, for managing emergencies or for handling the human interaction after unanticipated outcomes. In addition, equipment failure, often unrecognized as such and attributed to human error, as well as other unanticipated hazards, such as a patient falling from an examination table, can create allegations of malpractice. In fact, any number of conditions can contribute to an allegation of malpractice. Nevertheless, three defining factors contribute to whether litigation will be pursued and the outcome of such litigation:

1. The ultimate decision to sue is based on unmet expectations and poor communication between the provider (and staff) and the patient and/or the patient's family.[68]

2. Patients expect honesty and transparent communication.[69]

3. Documentation is a key factor on how well the suit can be defended. As the risk management mantra states, "If it isn't written, it didn't happen."[70]

■ Medical Service Delivery System

Diminished patient satisfaction results partially from the way health care is delivered. Patients want respect, as do those who deliver care. Waiting times, the method for making appointments, how reliably and efficiently patients flow through the system, and how rushed patients feel during appointments all affect the discrepancy between patient expectations and experience. This discrepancy is what evolves into dissatisfaction such that when something even minor goes wrong during care, the stage is set for anger and disappointment.[71]

Despite temptations to overbook patients to accommodate failures to show, a more realistic scheduling process that allows for variability in visit length based on need is ideal. Recognizing that the ideal will not always be met, a process for communicating with patients about delays in appointments or changes of schedule can address patient needs for timeliness and communication.

The patient flow process, just as any care process, should be diagrammed and evaluated for areas of potential communication failures, information "falling through cracks" in the system, and sources of patient dissatisfaction. The evaluation should consider such issues as time allotment per patient, management of walk-ins and emergencies, processes for appointment making, follow-up appointments, registration, and waiting room environment and time. Resources regarding patient flow are available through the Institute for Healthcare Improvement (IHI)[72] as well as other sources.

TASK 7 **Establish Patient, Staff, and Organizational Confidentiality Policies**

■ Federal, State, and Local Laws and Regulations

Key to confidentiality for patients are the administrative simplification provisions included in the Health Insurance Portability and Accountability Act of 1996 (HIPAA).[73] In addition to mandating national standards for several administrative transactions and identification numbers, HIPAA's privacy and security regulations limit the type of protected health information (PHI) that can be disclosed, to whom it can be disclosed, and how it can be disclosed, as well as outlining the steps needed to secure electronic health information at rest and in transit. HIPAA also requires that patients be notified of their rights under the act and be provided the opportunity to review, copy, and make corrections to their medical records. Other federal laws, such as those that protect substance abuse treatment records, and regulations about the safekeeping of medical information (e.g., bloodborne pathogen regulations under OSHA's regulations) add another layer of protection to patient privacy.[74] Furthermore, applicable state laws impacting patient privacy must be evaluated as more stringent state laws supersede HIPAA.

■ Organizational Information Flow

It is essential on many levels – risk management being one of the most important – that medical practices review internal processes to ensure compliance with HIPAA and other appropriate laws and regulations. All processes related to the handling, transmission, and storage of PHI should be flow-charted and analyzed. As an alternative, these processes could be evaluated through the use of a failure modes and effects analysis, specifically seeking to identify areas where there is the opportunity for breach of confidentiality of PHI. Areas that practices should focus on include:

- *Communication with patients.* Policies should address how communication with patients is handled by mail, e-mail, and telephone, as well as what procedures to use for communication of information to patients' families and friends. In addition, policies should be implemented to limit the disclosure of PHI in waiting rooms and public areas of the practice.

- *Check-in and checkout.* Specific procedures should address how patient privacy is handled at check-in so that the opportunity for others to overhear conversations with patients at the desk is minimized. Hard-copy medical records and computer screens containing patient information should be kept away from incoming patients and placed in such a way that patient identifiers are not readily visible.

- *Staff training.* All practice staff, including volunteers, must be fully trained in protecting the confidentiality and security of medical records. It is also recommended that staff be re-trained on a periodic basis.

- *Billing procedures and use of third parties.* Billing procedures should fully comply with HIPAA. Practices must comply with the "minimum necessary" provision of the privacy regulation by transmitting only the specific health information requested by health plans. (The minimum necessary provision does not apply, however, when the practice sends PHI to another provider for treatment purposes.) Practices for which

PHI is handled by noncovered entities (e.g., data storage companies, transcription services, and shredding vendors) must ensure that the appropriate business associate agreements are in place and that practice procedures support appropriate transmission of PHI.

- *De-identification of PHI.* Any report generated by the practice that may contain patient identifiers should be scrutinized to ensure that it complies with HIPAA in both use and structure. Whenever possible, PHI that is used for aggregation purposes should be de-identified. Uses of reports or marketing materials that include PHI and that do not have patient release forms are also limited under HIPAA. Risk managers must ensure that reports are being used only for quality purposes; peer review and/or credentialing purposes; or insurance, medical, legal, auditing, cost management, or management/business purposes as defined in the HIPAA Privacy Rule.[75]

- *Documentation.* It is recommended that practices document all practice policies and procedures relating to the privacy and security of PHI, including staff training sessions. In addition, all patient privacy form acknowledgments should be documented. In the case of patients who were unable to or refused to sign, a record should be kept of the date when the notice was offered or sent to them.

■ Policies and Procedures

Practices must develop policies and procedures that adhere to HIPAA's privacy and security regulations. HIPAA provides a broad outline of how a practice can comply – each organization is permitted to take into account its culture and technical capabilities as it crafts its policies and procedures. A practice's privacy and security policies and procedures should address not only traditional medical records, but also all records that contain PHI, including appointment records, billing records, telephone message records, and any other system in the practice that utilizes PHI. It must be made clear to all staff exactly who can release information and under what cir-cumstances, as well as the procedures for documenting all releases of information. In addition, policies should state how subpoenas for production of records are to be handled, including subpoenas for in-court testimony.

HIPAA training should be part of each new employee's orienta-tion. Frequent in-service and annual reminder training should be part of the practice's competency and continuing-education process. HIPAA touches on the daily work of the practice and is an area where inadvertent and well-intended actions can easily lead to an unintended breach. It is in the purview of the medical practice executive to reduce the risk of such a consequence.

In many medical groups, the practice administrator has the responsibility to ensure the organization is in compliance with all appropriate laws and regulations. The complex and comprehensive nature of the HIPAA privacy and security regulations make these important and challenging risk management issues.

TASK 8 # Conduct Audits of At-Risk Financial Activities

■ Federal, State, and Local Tax Codes

Just like personal income taxes, the tax codes that apply to businesses change regularly. Whether the organization is classified as nonprofit or for-profit, there is no reasonable way for the medical practice executive to remain on top of all pertinent codes in a functional manner. The nonprofit organization has certain criteria it must meet to maintain its nonprofit status, which sets it apart from the for-profit organization. The medical practice executive should ensure that s/he keeps apprised of any ongoing continuing-education courses and reading material that is available. Ultimately, a relationship with a certified public accountant who specializes in the type of corporate structure employed by the organization is the best risk management.

■ Generally Accepted Accounting Principles

Although a variety of approaches to accounting standards in business exist, most companies use what is known as generally accepted accounting principles (GAAP). GAAP is a system of accounting that encompasses a set of rules and procedures for presenting and auditing information. The universal application of this method makes it the industry standard. It is applicable to both for-profit and nonprofit tax structures and is applicable in health care, although it has some characteristics that may not be suitable to health care organizations. For example, the GAAP method does not permit health care organizations to report charity care as either an expense or a negative offset to income. Charity care is reported only as a footnote. This artificially inflates apparent income by not accounting for the financial cost of charity care. Additionally, contractual adjustments cannot be reported as a reduction in net revenue, again artificially inflating revenue to the detriment of the health care organization. Although these and other principles of GAAP may be insufficient to explore other types of financial accounting, it is important that organization leaders and the board fully appreciate the implications and uses of GAAP data.[76]

■ Systems Analysis Models and Procedures

Ultimately, risk management is a financial management process. Therefore, it is essential that the medical practice executive have a working knowledge of basic systems analysis tools. Financial models and forecasting models are available through texts and management information products. Profit and loss reporting, balance sheets, and cash flow projections help the executive gain a complete picture of the financial health of the organization. In addition, software products that manage the organization's accounting information can generate forecasting reports that can assist the nonfinancial executive in conducting an analysis without the need to understand the theory supporting the model.

■ Accounting and Auditing Systems

Computer programs designed for organizations of specific sizes are also available to run accounting and cost analysis reports. Software is available for in-house application by staff. Many of these software packages include applications for report sharing with external accountants and auditors. In addition, Web-based companies exist that generate industry comparisons for benchmarking. Organizations should look for software appropriate to the nature and size of the practice. Online resources, such as the "Tax and Accounting Sites Directory," are a starting place for software evaluation.[77]

Tax Reports and Returns

Although the general public is increasingly using computer programs to calculate and submit taxes, it is probably not a good idea for a health care practice. Liability for accuracy is inherent in tax preparation. Unless the medical executive is current on all applicable tax laws and the fine points of applicability for the type of organizational and tax structure of the organization, the preparation of taxes is best left to a tax specialist. For the health care practice, that specialist should be knowledgeable of any unique tax issues faced by the organization.

Reports

Reports are a management tool, or specifically, a risk management tool. The careful review and evaluation of exception reports, cost reports, forecasts, and tax estimates can reveal loss exposures that are apparent only when viewed in aggregate. One hospital had a billing process that automatically charged a new service to the last insurance billed unless the insurance was manually changed at each visit. During the course of one year, the hospital's health insurance plan had been charged for more than $123,000 of workers' compensation bills. Health insurance plan costs were increasing while workers' compensation costs remained low. Because of the way billing reports were generated, this situation went unnoticed until the risk manager suspected a discrepancy in the number of services provided and the amount of charges being generated through workers' compensation. In addition, a charge for a mammogram appeared in a workers' compensation loss run. This led the risk manager to request a special report, which revealed the substantial error and led to a process review. In this case, a process correction occurred because of a carefully reviewed report.

TASK 9 # Develop Professional Resource Networks for Risk-Related Activities

■ Consultative Resources

Every practice has a wealth of internal knowledge and expertise. However, few practices have knowledge and expertise about every business, legal, and financial issue. The business of the medical practice is the delivery of health care. The medical practice executive is charged with having sufficient knowledge to manage the daily operations and with knowing when outside help is required. The use of outside help, however, is costly, but the lack of use of appropriate outside help could be even costlier if an issue is not handled properly.

To develop appropriate professional resources, the medical practice executive must recognize those high-risk areas where outside consultants may be useful. Most often, the areas of business that are complex are fraught with potential for great financial loss, and those that change rapidly and regularly are those for which a resource network is most likely useful. Using that reasoning, such a network would include:

- *Attorneys.* Individual attorneys might be needed for consultation on medical malpractice, employment liability issues, union issues, mergers and acquisitions, tax issues, corporate structure and corporate law, environmental issues, real estate, compliance, workers' compensation, and general corporate concerns.

- *Accountants.* Accountants often specialize in the areas of tax, captive management, foundation management, trusts, Medicare/Medicaid, and other business endeavors.

- *Tax specialists.* Beyond the accountant and attorney are consultants who specialize in tax structures and in maximizing tax advantages. For large organizations or organizations with both nonprofit and for-profit businesses under an umbrella structure, a tax specialist could be a useful consultant.

- *Financial advisors.* Financial advisors assist the organization with making investments that are allowable under Medicare/Medicaid regulations and are in accordance with the practice's corporate and tax structure.

- *Insurance brokers.* As mentioned previously in this volume, an experienced insurance broker is essential for ensuring that the organization develops a comprehensive risk-financing program that addresses the known exposures. The organization may choose to use the services of one broker, or it may have multiple brokers for different lines of coverage expertise.

- *Environmental consultant.* Although the practice may have appropriate mechanisms for disposal of hazardous waste and may not incinerate or generate gases, there may still be environmental concerns related to assumption of responsibility for previous owners of the property or for the environmental impact of new construction. An environmental consultation is sometimes recommended when participating in a merger or acquisition or in a divestment of property.

The need for consultants changes with the needs of the organization. Because this is a fluid area, it is important that the medical practice executive be clear about recruiting, working with, and retaining experts. Due diligence on the credentials and credibility of consultants is highly recommended.

■ Contract Negotiations with Consultants

The medical practice executive must be clear about the level of expertise it expects and requires for the job to be done. The contract should clearly state the medical practice's expectations about the nature and level of expertise to be provided. In addition, contracts should clearly state the amount and type of service to be delivered and the expected time frame for deliverables. Consultants will generally attempt to shift all liability for outcome to the medical practice under the rationale that it ultimately decides how much of the consultant's advice to implement. It is important that the contract be reviewed carefully to ensure that there is not an undue burden being placed on the practice to accept liability for acts of the consultant over which it has no control. In the end, the medical practice executive must weigh the risks of consultant use against the benefits. Although costly to use, the time, energy, and expertise gained through outsourcing complex high-risk activities may outweigh the cost and the headache.[78]

■ Current and Future Risk-Related Issues

Often the resource network consists of relationships that are activated on an as-needed basis. Rather than entering into single contract projects, the practice may choose to have certain consultants on retainer, or may choose to have periodic interactions between contractual projects. These types of relationships frequently emerge naturally with time and positive working encounters. Nevertheless, the practice may desire to cultivate certain relationships based on its specific needs. Recognition of past needs for specialists in communication, medical records, or information systems may generate a need to maintain ongoing relationships with consultants in any given area. For example, a current litigation may awaken the practice to realize that the high-risk birth program has some unaddressed exposures. Perhaps the risk assessment of the patient flow process demonstrates areas of latent exposure to communication breakdown that could lead to a system failure, medical error, and patient injury. Consultant relationships can improve the practice's operation when the consultant fits the organization's culture and philosophical approach to health care.

Negotiate and Comply with Contractual Arrangements

■ Contract Negotiation

Contract negotiation is a complex activity. Contracts create legally binding obligations between two parties. Every contract is unique and requires careful consideration. The nature of the contract dictates the components that are most critical. Contracts with payers will focus on protection of PHI, agreed amount of payment, time frame for payment, billing procedures, accessibility to other records, risk transfer, and more. Contracts with physicians, however, will be significantly different. With a physician the practice is concerned about level of expertise and the maintenance of that expertise, the amount of work, and the nature of the work, as well as agreed-upon compensation.

Issues such as benefits and compensation plan contingencies will be a large component of the contract, as may noncompete clauses or other business agreements. Transfer of risk may not be an issue if the practice is going to provide professional liability insurance. If such insurance is not provided by the practice, the contract should specify the amount of expected coverage and the frequency for providing proof of insurance. With contractors and vendors, the terms are often more concrete. The deliverables are usually goods or specific services and the issues of transfer of risk are even greater. Some specific components are critical to all contracts:

- Parties are named;

- Expectations for performance are delineated;

- The length of the contract and the date of its termination are stipulated;

- The insurance requirements and indemnification requirements are delineated;

- How the contract gets amended is specified;

- The choice of law governing the contract is defined; and

- Whether the contract can be assigned is addressed.

Other provisions might include review of records, any exhibits or appendices, and conditions for alternative dispute resolution.[79]

■ Health Care Law

All contracts entered into by the practice should be reviewed to ensure they comply with applicable health care laws. Practices that accept federal funds need to be particularly careful that no conditions of participation or regulations applicable to recipients of federal monies are violated. Physicians must be educated about the implications of Stark I and II and the anti-kickback laws. In addition, legal counsel should be queried not only about the contract conditions themselves, but also whether the contract sets up any potential conflicts that could be seen as antitrust, Stark, or anti-kickback violations.

The medical practice as an entity is not the only party at risk. Through peer discussion and education by legal counsel, physician members of the practice group need to understand the implications of their personal investment in companies that might be perceived as creating a Stark or other legal conflict with their role in the practice. No business contract related to health care services should be entered by either the organization or its member physicians without a careful review by legal counsel to avoid complicated allegations of improper acts.

■ Needs Assessment

Contracts are binding legal documents, and as such they should not be considered lightly. If a contract is not necessary, perhaps there are situations in which it should be avoided. Contract negotiation is a skill. The more experience the medical practice executive accumulates, the more astute s/he will become at identifying potential exposures created through contractual language. The medical practice executive bearing the risk management responsibility should consider:

- The organization's past contractual experience – whether with a potential contractor or with others;

- The present situation – whether it warrants a contractual agreement or if it could be best served in another way;

- The future needs of the organization – whether this is a long-term relationship that might be better served as an employment relationship or if this need is a short-term one that warrants a limited relationship;

- The competitive advantages to having this relationship – whether the practice gains knowledge, expertise, or a unique approach; and

- The trends in the field – whether using this service is going to move the organization toward its long-term competitive goals.

TASK 11 Maintain Compliance with Government Contractual Mandates

■ Contract Law

Recipients of federal monies must comply with specific laws related to the reporting of activity, the nature of contractual relationships, and the regulations pertaining to employees and employment. A prudent risk management strategy involves working with an attorney familiar with federal contracting requirements. In addition, the medical practice executive should strive to keep abreast of the most current information provided through CMS and other information sources. CMS provides regular updates for physicians and health care organizations. In addition, Web subscriptions, such as Government Policy News-links,[80] scan all federal publications daily searching for changes and significant postings. These scanning services send out a daily link to all important information. Although there is a significant amount of information not directly related to government contracting, other types of pertinent health care information, including the *Federal Register*, provide the medical practice executive with up-to-date information on trends.

■ Federal, State, and Local Laws and Regulations

In addition to law specific to contracts, other state, federal, and local laws influence compliance. As described in Task 1, the purpose of compliance programs is to ensure adherence to federal regulation. Although they apply to the organization's relationship with employees, OSHA regulations, the Family Medical Leave Act, and the Americans with Disabilities Act are all part of the corporate compliance program. Consequently, compliance with these regulations is implied in the acceptance of federal funds.

Self-Referral Laws and Regulations

As described in Task 1, violations of Stark I and II and the anti-kickback laws are clearly infringements of federal compliance standards. Physicians must be educated about the implications of these laws on what they may consider to be their private investments or business. Policies and procedures should clearly delineate acceptable and nonacceptable business practices, including the size and nature of gifts that can be accepted, the types of business transactions that are allowed, and the process for reporting concerns or questions. The medical practice executive should regularly monitor the business activities of the practice's physicians to ensure there is no conflict.

Fraud and Abuse Laws and Regulations

Long thought of as the heart of compliance programs, Medicare billing practices are a huge portion of federal compliance and an implied agreement of federal contracting. The practice has a responsibility to ensure that physicians understand proper coding and billing processes as well as documentation standards commensurate with Medicare billing. Furthermore, the practice should have policies in place that are enforced as well as regularly provided training for documentation for proper billing.

■ Record-Keeping

Similar to patient records and other business records, as discussed in Task 2, records of government contracts and all aspects of the corporate compliance program should be maintained in accordance with contract specifications and with the federal regulations relevant to each specific federal act.

Conclusion

RISK MANAGEMENT is a comprehensive set of management skills that covers the entire spectrum of activity in the practice. It is not a function; rather, it is a management skill and process that, if used correctly, can identify areas of potential loss long before they emerge. Risk management draws on federal and state legislation and regulation as well as principles of safety science, principles of communication and human interaction, and business practices. It creates a network of measurements against which the daily operation of the medical practice can benchmark itself to find the means to reduce injury to patients and employees and to minimize financial loss to the health care organization.

Exercises

THESE QUESTIONS have been retired from the ACMPE Essay Exam question bank. Because there are so many ways to handle various situations, there are no "right" answers, and thus, no answer key. Use these questions to help you practice responses in different scenarios.

1. You are the administrator of a medical group practice that outsources its transcriptions. You have signed a business associate agreement with the transcription service. A local attorney's office that uses the same transcription service has just notified you that they mistakenly received and opened a batch of your practice's transcriptions.

   Describe how you would handle this situation.

2. You are the new administrator of a specialty group practice
    with a 50-percent Medicare patient population. You are
    made aware that one physician in particular has not dic-
    tated consultation reports back to the referring physicians
    for up to one year. The practice has, however, billed and
    been paid for these consultations. You are concerned about
    the compliance issues surrounding this problem.

    Describe how you would handle this situation.

3. You are the administrator of a small medical practice. You
    and the physicians recently attended a meeting at which
    Medicare fraud and abuse was a hot topic. The physicians
    are now convinced that a compliance program is needed in
    their practice and have asked you to develop one.

    Describe how you would develop, implement, and monitor
    the compliance program.

4. You are the administrator of a medical group. A patient has
    contacted you, claiming that his outstanding bill is the
    result of incorrect billing practices, and the billing office is
    unwilling to correct the invoice. The patient has contacted
    his attorney about filing a complaint with the Board of
    Medical Examiners, as well as filing a consumer fraud
    claim.

    Describe how you would handle this situation.

5. You are the administrator for a 10-physician group practice.
    Two weeks ago, a physician's nurse resigned to accept a
    position at another clinic. Today you received, by registered
    mail, a notice from the Equal Employment Opportunity
    Commission (EEOC) stating that the former employee has
    filed a charge of discrimination against the practice. She
    alleges that she was sexually harassed by the physician
    with whom she worked.

    Explain how you would handle this situation.

6. You are the administrator of a large multispecialty group.
    At the last board of director's monthly meeting, your group
    adopted a compliance plan proposed by the compliance
    committee. The compliance committee is made up of five
    senior members who volunteered for the committee. A
    number of physicians are noncompliant with the plan. The
    pediatricians in the group feel there is no need for them to
    meet the plan guidelines because they do not treat
    Medicare patients. The two rheumatologists in the group,
    who are not compliance committee members, do not feel
    they have to meet the plan guidelines either. Two cardiolo-
    gists who serve on the compliance committee want to
    know if they will get extra compensation if they meet the
    compliance plan guidelines.

    Describe how you would handle this situation.

7. You are the administrator of a midsize primary care prac-
    tice that recently had to eliminate several positions due to
    declining reimbursements. You receive an anonymous
    response to an exit interview questionnaire from a former
    employee. The document states that the employee had
    concerns about inappropriate behavior in the practice.
    The employee shared that one of the doctors routinely
    upcoded, that all employees and physicians were aware of
    the situation, and that no one responded to concerns about
    this wrongdoing. You bring this complaint to the compli-
    ance officer, who is concerned that the former employee
    may become a whistleblower.

    Describe how you would handle this situation.

Notes

1. G. L. Head & S. Horn, *Essentials of Risk Management*, Vol. 1 (Malvern, Pa.: Insurance Institute of America, 1991), 1.

2. J. McCaffrey & S. Hagg-Rickert, "Development of a Risk Management Program," in R. Carroll (ed.), *The Risk Management Handbook for Healthcare Organizations* (San Francisco: Jossey-Bass, 2004), 95.

3. W. R. Ching, "Enterprise Risk Management: Laying a Broader Framework for Health Care Risk Management," in R. Carroll (ed.), *The Risk Management Handbook for Healthcare Organizations* (San Francisco: Jossey-Bass, 2004), 3.

4. G. L. Head & S. Horn, *Essentials of Risk Management*, Vol. 1, 6.

5. J. Reason, *Human Error* (Cambridge, U.K.: Cambridge University Press, 1990), 208.

6. K. B. Thomas, "New Orleans Today: It's Worse Than You Think," *Time* (November 20, 2005).

7. J. Reason, *Human Error*, 208.

8. R. E. McDermott, R. J. Mikulak, & M. R. Beauregard, *The Basics of FMEA* (Portland, Ore.: Productivity, Inc., 1996), 1–5.

9. G. L. Head & S. Horn, *Essentials of Risk Management*, Vol. 1, 8.

10. G. L. Head & S. Horn, *Essentials of Risk Management*, Vol. 2 (Malvern, Pa.: Insurance Institute of America, 1991), 13.

11. For more information, see the "Patient and Provider Education Materials" section on the Centers for Disease Control Website, www.cdc.gov/flu/professionals/patiented.htm.

12. For information on infection control recommendations for pandemic influenza, see "Supplement 4 Infection Control" on the HHS Website, www.hhs.gov/pandemicflu/plan/sup4.html.

13. For more information, see "Surge Capacity" in "Supplement 3 Healthcare Planning" on the HHS Website, www.hhs.gov/pandemicflu/plan/sup3.html#surge.

14. House Committee on Science, World Trade Center, "Lessons Learned from Ground Zero," www.house.gov/science/wtc.htm (retrieved March 7, 2002).

15. K. R. Roberts, K. Yu, & D. V. Stralen, "Patient Safety Is an Organizational Systems Issue: Lessons from a Variety of Industries," in B. Youngberg & M. Hatlie (eds.), *The Patient Safety Handbook* (Sudbury, Mass.: Jones and Bartlett, 2004), 171–173.

16. Ibid.

17. G. Porto, "Creating Patient Safety and High Reliability," in R. Carroll (ed.), *The Risk Management Handbook for Healthcare Organizations* (San Francisco: Jossey-Bass, 2004), 322.

18. G. L. Head & S. Horn, *Essentials of Risk Management*, Vol. 2, 40.

19. Ibid., 162.

20. American College of Medical Practice Executives (ACMPE), *The ACMPE Guide to the Body of Knowledge for Medical Practice Management* (Englewood, Colo.: American College of Medical Practice Executives, 2003), 76.

21. Ibid., 77.

22. 45 CFR Parts 160 and 164. Regulation text available at www.hhs.gov/ocr/combinedregtext.pdf.

23. G. L. Imperato, M. Segal, & L. J. Perling, "Legal Implications of Business Arrangements in the Health Care Industry," in L. F. Wolper (ed.), *Physician Practice Management* (Sudbury, Mass.: Jones and Bartlett, 2005), 471.

24. G. D. Pozgar, *Legal Aspects of Health Care Administration*. (Sudbury, Mass.: Jones and Bartlett, 2004), 474.

25. B. A. Johnson, "Medical Practice and Compensation Plans," in L. F. Wolper (ed.), *Physician Practice Management* (Sudbury, Mass.: Jones and Bartlett, 2005), 559.

26. R. A. Havlisch, "Emerging Liabilities in Partnerships, Joint Ventures, and Collaborative Relationships," in R. Carroll (ed.), *The Risk Management Handbook for Healthcare Organizations* (San Francisco: Jossey-Bass, 2004), 695.

27. Federal Trade Commission, *Antitrust Guidelines for Collaborations Among Competitors*, www.ftc.gov/os/2000/04/ftcdojguidelines.pdf.

28. Anti-Kickback Statute, codified as Criminal Penalties for Acts Involving Federal Health Care Programs, U.S. Code 42, §1320a-7b.

29. Ibid., §1320a-7a.

30. S. K. Sledge & H. A. Pierson, *Silicon Valley/San Jose Business Journal*, January 20, 1998, www.bizjournals.com/sanjose/stories/1998/02/02/focus2.html.

31. J. E. Driver & G. T. Troyer, "Corporate Compliance – A Risk Management Framework," in R. Carroll (ed.), *The Risk Management Handbook for Healthcare Organizations* (San Francisco: Jossey-Bass, 2004), 1105.

32. P. J. White, "Employment Practices Legal Issues," in R. Carroll (ed.), *The Risk Management Handbook for Healthcare Organizations* (San Francisco: Jossey-Bass, 2004), 873.

33. G. Amori, "Office Practice Risk Management," in L. F. Wolper (ed.), *Physician Practice Management* (Sudbury, Mass.: Jones and Bartlett, 2005), 432.

34. Free Management Library, Authenticity Consulting, LLC, "Some Legal Considerations for Board Members," www.managementhelp.org/legal/lgl_thot.htm.

35. J. McCaffrey & S. Hagg-Rickert, "Development of a Risk Management Program," 104.

36. J. Horty & M. Hanslovan, "Governance of the Health Care Organization," in R. Carroll (ed.), *The Risk Management Handbook for Healthcare Organizations* (San Francisco: Jossey-Bass, 2004), 83.

37. Safe Medical Device Act of 1990 (SMDA), U.S. Code 21 §360i(a).

38. Ibid., 360i(a)(6).

39. *HHS/OIG Compliance Program Guidance for Hospitals*, p. 4, www.oig.hhs.gov/authorities/docs/cpghosp.pdf.

40. HHS Office of Inspector General, *Compliance Guidance*, www.oig.hhs.gov/fraud/complianceguidance.html.

41. K. S. Davis, J. C. McConnell, & E. D. Shaw, "Data Management," in R. Carroll (ed.), *The Risk Management Handbook for Healthcare Organizations* (San Francisco: Jossey-Bass, 2004), 1220.

42. G. D. Pozgar, *Legal Aspects*, 434–435.

43. National Labor Relations Act of 1935 (NLRA), U.S. Code 29 §151 et seq.

44. P. J. White, "Employment Practices Legal Issues," 861.

45. *NLRB v. Weingarten, Inc.*, 420 U.S. 251, 88 LRRM 2689 (1975).

46. Title VII of the Civil Rights Act of 1964, U.S. Code 42, §2000e et seq.

47. Age Discrimination in Employment Act of 1967, U.S. Code 29, §621 et seq.

48. 42 U.S.C. §2000e-5(a)–(g)

49. G. D. Pozgar, *Legal Aspects*, 456.

50. Conditions of Participation for Hospitals, 42 CFR§482.13.

51. Fair Labor Standards Act, U.S. Code 29, Ch. 8, §201 et seq.

52. Equal Pay Act of 1963, U.S. Code 29, §206(d)(1) et seq.

53. Title VII of the Civil Rights Act of 1964, 29 CFR Part 1604.11.

54. Americans with Disabilities Act of 1990, U.S. Code 42, §12101 et seq.

55. Occupational Safety and Health Act (1970), Public Law 91-596, Codified at U.S. Code 29, §651-678.

56. U.S. Department of Labor, Occupational Safety and Health Administration, OSHA Act of 1970, www.osha.gov/pls/oshaweb/owadisp.show_document? p_table=OSHACT&p_id=2743.

57. K. M. McPhaul & J. A. Lipscomb, "Workplace Violence in Health Care: Recognized but Not Regulated," *Online Journal of Issues in Nursing* 9, no. 3 (2004), Manuscript 6. Available at www.nursingworld.org/ojin/topic25/ tpc25_6.htm.

58. F. Kavaler & A. D. Spiegel, "Assuring Safety and Security in Health Care Institutions," in F. K. Kavaler & A. D. Spiegel (eds.), *Risk Management in Health Care Institutions: A Strategic Approach* (Sudbury, Mass.: Jones and Bartlett, 2003), 198–201.

59. OSHA Publication, 4138-01R.

60. Occupational Safety and Health Administration, "Guidelines for Preventing Workplace Violence for Health Care & Social Service Workers," www.osha.gov/Publications/osha3148.pdf.

61. Drug Free Workplace Act of 1988, U.S. Code 41, §701.

62. P. J. White, "Employment Practices Legal Issues," 873.

63. P. D. Stergios, et al., "Labor and Employment Laws Applicable to Physicians' Practices," in L. F. Wolper (ed.), *Physician Practice Management* (Sudbury, Mass.: Jones and Bartlett, 2005), 536-538.

64. Drug Abuse Prevention, Treatment, and Rehabilitation Act, 42 CFR Part 2.

65. B. H. Bussell, "Managed Care," in R. Carroll (ed.), *The Risk Management Handbook for Healthcare Organizations* (San Francisco: Jossey-Bass, 2004), 517–520.

66. Ibid., 536.

67. G. Amori, "Communication with Patients and Other Customers: The Ultimate Loss Control Tool," in R. Carroll (ed.), *The Risk Management Handbook for Healthcare Organizations* (San Francisco: Jossey-Bass, 2004), 821.

68. C. Vincent, M. Young, & A. Phillips, "Why Do People Sue Doctors? A Study of Patient and Relatives Taking Legal Action," *Lancet* 343, no. 8913 (1994): 1609–1613.

69. G. Amori, "Communication with Patients," 821.

70. Anonymous.

71. S. K. Baker, *Managing Patient Expectations: The Art of Finding and Keeping Loyal Patients* (San Francisco: Jossey-Bass, 1999).

72. Institute for Healthcare Improvement, www.ihi.org/ihi.

73. Health Insurance Portability and Accountability Act of 1996 (HIPAA), Codified at 45 CFR Parts 160 and 164. See "Standards for Privacy of Individually Identifiable Health Information, Security Standards for the Protection of Electronic Protected Health Information, and General Administrative Requirements," available on the Dept. of Health and Human Services Website at www.hhs.gov/ocr/combinedregtext.pdf.

74. R. Glitz & C. L. Stanton, "The Health Insurance Portability and Accountability Act (HIPAA) of 1996," in R. Carroll (ed.), *The Risk Management Handbook for Healthcare Organizations* (San Francisco: Jossey-Bass, 2004), 1130.

75. Privacy of Individually Identifiable Information, 45 CFR §164.501.

76. D. N. Gans & S. M. Andes, "Accounting and Budgeting for Medical Practice Managers," in L. F. Wolper (ed.), *Physician Practice Management* (Sudbury, Mass.: Jones and Bartlett, 2004), 235–236.

77. "Tax and Accounting Sites Directory," accounting software, www.taxsites.com/software2.html.

78. P. A. Nakamura, "Contract Review Primer for Risk Managers," in R. Carroll (ed.), *The Risk Management Handbook for Healthcare Organizations* (San Francisco: Jossey-Bass, 2004), 500.

79. Ibid., 489–491.

80. Government Policy Newslinks, available at http://policynewslinks.com.

About the Author

Geraldine Amori, PhD, ARM, CPHRM, is a nationally known speaker, facilitator, and consultant on risk management and communication issues in health care and patient safety. Her clients have included Voluntary Hospitals of America, Harvard Risk Management Foundation, and AIG Consultants, Inc. Dr. Amori is the past president of both the American Society for Healthcare Risk Management (ASHRM) and the Northern New England Society for Healthcare Risk Management. She has more than 25 years of experience in health care, serving in mental health services as well as in health care administration. For 12 of those years, Dr. Amori served as risk manager at Fletcher Allen Health in Burlington, Vermont, where she developed expertise in office practice risk management, workers' compensation, and captive operations. She is the author of "Communicating with Patients and Families," a chapter in the 4th edition of the *Risk Management Handbook* (ASHRM). In addition, she is the primary author of the Disclosure Monograph Series for ASHRM, as well as the author of a risk management chapter in *Physician Practice Management*, a book co-branded by MGMA.

Dr. Amori is an active member of the National Speakers Association and a former member of the board of directors of Vermont Stage Company. In addition, she has served on the American Hospital Association (AHA) Quality Quest Patient Safety Award Committee and is a member of the Partnership for Patient Safety (p4ps) Advisory Group, and the board of directors of Consumers Advancing Patient Safety. Dr. Amori has also been a member of the Health Forum/AHA Patient Safety Fellowship Advisory Committee.

Index